KAIZEN
AND
THE ART OF
CREATIVE
THINKING

KAIZEN
AND
THE ART OF
CREATIVE
THINKING

THE SCIENTIFIC THINKING MECHANISM
SHIGEO SHINGO

Originally published as *Idea wo Nigasuna*, copyright 1959 by Hakuto-Shobo Publishing Company, Tokyo, Japan.

English translation © 2007 by Enna Products Corporation and PCS Inc.

Enna Products Corporation
1602 Carolina St.
Unit B3
Bellingham, WA 98229
Telephone: (360) 306-5369
Fax: (905) 481-0756
E-mail: info@enna.com

PCS Inc.
809 S.E. 73rd Ave.
Vancouver, WA 98664
Telephone: (360) 737-1883
Fax: (360) 737-1940
E-mail: info@pcspress.com

Printed in the United States of America

Library of Congress Control Number: 2007935987

Library of Congress Cataloging-in-Publication Data
Shingo, Shigeo, 1909-1990
Kaizen and the Art of Creative Thinking
    Includes index.
    ISBN 978-1-897363-59-1

    1. Lean Manufacturing 2. Idea generation. 3. Improvement initiatives

THE SHINGO PRIZE: CELEBRATING 20 YEARS

As Shigeo's Shingo publisher I have known of Dr. Shingo's contribution to the world of manufacturing for many years. I have often thought he was entitled to a Nobel Prize; in fact I contacted the Nobel representative in the United States, but was told that there was no category for Dr. Shingo's work. I knew it was not true for there is a Nobel Prize in Economics, and without a doubt Dr. Shingo's work has saved the world billions of dollars, and will continue to do so.

A few months after I contacted the people with Nobel, I met Dr. Vernon M. Buehler, a professor at Utah State University. I spoke at a conference at the school. While in conversation with Vern, he asked me if I could get Shingo to speak at his next conference, I said yes, but with conditions. I said we needed to get Shingo an honorary Doctorate degree. Vern said that he couldn't guarantee it but that he would do all that was necessary to apply for one. In discussions together, we then decided that America needed a manufacturing prize similar to the Deming Prize. In Japan, Japanese companies fiercely compete for the coveted Deming Prize. Dr. Deming taught statistical process control and taught how companies could improve quality. The Japanese listened; we did not.

Based on the success of the Deming Prize in Japan, Vern and I thought that an American manufacturing prize might spur on American industry to "wake–up" to the international challenges. We both thought, based on the discoveries of Shingo, that it would be appropriate to name the American prize after him.

Vern and I then invited a group of senior American executives to form the initial board of directors of the prize. Shingo and I contributed $50,000 for the start of the prize and Vern got Utah State University's Partners in Business to initially sponsor the prize.

The board set up the criteria for the prize and sent out request notices to American industry. At the time, as president of Productivity Inc. and Productivity Press, I had an enormous mailing list to solicit applications. I remember, close to a year later, we had received around a dozen applications for the prize. At that board meeting we reviewed and discussed which companies were worthy of winning the initial prize. One board member was adamant that no company was worthy of winning the prize. He said, "No company has passed the criteria set for productivity improvement." I chimed in, "look we have a prize; we must have a winner." It was a fierce discussion. I told the group to take a break and since Shingo was there to speak at the conference, I went to get his advice. He said, "Norman, you treat the prize just like a beauty contest and give it to the best company." With Shingo's powerful statement, it was easy for me to convince all of the other delegates, but one, that we would pick out the best company to win the prize.

We did and the prize has only been growing stronger every year these past 20 years.

And subsequently, Vern delivered. Utah State University did award Shingo an honorary doctorate degree. I remember the moment very clearly. Even though it was very difficult for

Shingo to walk at the time, he did and participated in all of the processions. As the honorary doctorate degree was awarded he gave a brilliant speech to the auditorium filled with students, teachers, friends and families. It was Dr. Shingo's proudest moment.

When he died less than a year later, his wife placed his cap and gown around him and displayed him that way for the funeral ceremonies.

Dr. Shingo was probably the greatest manufacturing consultant of the last 100 years. I am still indebted to Utah State University for recognizing the contributions of Dr. Shingo to American industry.

Co-publisher,

Norman Bodek

ADVANCED PRAISE FOR
KAIZEN AND THE ART OF CREATIVE THINKING

"In this book we learn how Dr. Shingo thinks about problems. You will not be overwhelmed by flowery prose and deep theoretical discussions in a Shingo book; what you will get is a straightforward methodology and examples to illustrate each concept."

> Jeffrey Liker
> Ph.D., Industrial and Operations Engineering
> The University of Michigan

"This book contains a myriad of case studies taken from office examples as well as shop floors. It is a gold mine of improvement ideas that cumulatively must have saved millions, and will still do so today!"

> Don Dewar
> President & Founder
> Quality Digest Magazine

"Practicing kaizen (the habit of making small improvements) eludes many people. Dr. Shingo's Scientific Thinking Mechanism replaces the hope of the flash of creativity with a reliable and learnable habit–building approach. Thanks for making this Rosetta Stone for kaizen available to the world."

> Hal Macomber
> Principal
> Lean Project Consulting, Inc.

Advanced Praise for
Kaizen and the Art of Creative Thinking

ADVANCED PRAISE FOR
KAIZEN AND THE ART OF CREATIVE THINKING

"This book is great. Norman Bodek has discovered another goldmine of information for us to enjoy. Shingo's earlier books were real masterpieces that described in detail the techniques and the principles behind each revolutionary practice of the Toyota Production System. They were a real windfall to practitioners of Lean as they distilled decades of knowledge and presented it with a large number of actual examples making it easy to assimilate and apply. This book goes a step further as it deals with the thinking process that underlies Shingo's genius. I think this is just what the Lean movement needs to help it spread beyond manufacturing, and into other sectors such as services and healthcare."

T.V. Suresh
President
Tao Consultants

"For those of us who have revered the work of Dr. Shingo, this is an exciting work. More so than any other of his books, *Kaizen and the Art of Creative Thinking* gives us insight into the 'how' of Dr. Shingo's developments and accomplishments. His perspective is based in practical, real–world opportunities, not encumbered by complex theory and management rhetoric."

Bill Kluck
President
Northwest Lean Network

TABLE OF CONTENTS

Foreword

Shigeo Shingo has been in the background in most discussions of the Toyota Production System (TPS). Many who know of Dr. Shingo think of him as the man who contributed to rapid die exchange (SMED). It is clear that Taiichi Ohno was in charge of developing TPS at Toyota and he utilized Dr. Shingo's help in creating TPS. It is also clear that Dr. Shingo goes much deeper than SMED.

Shingo was a true Industrial Engineer (IE). He had a deep understanding of industrial processes and also contributed to the conceptual underpinnings of the Toyota Production System. TPS is, as *The Machine that Changed the World* declared, a different paradigm altogether than mass production. Traditional industrial engineering was very much steeped in mass production thinking. Many of the tools of I.E. were the underlying tools of TPS—standardized work, eliminating wasted motion, laying out the workplace to eliminate waste, and laying out the factory for flow. However, below the surface there were some subtle but critical differences in philosophy.

The philosophy of I.E. was based on a machine model—the factory is a machine and people are interchangeable parts of the machine. Get the design of the machine right and figure out scientifically the one best way for the person to do the job and direct the person to do it — punishing deviations from the design and rewarding compliance. These were the principles of Frederick Taylor's "Scientific Management" and very much reflect Western engineering thinking.

Dr. Shingo naturally gravitated toward the TPS philosophy rooted in the East. The factory is viewed as a system of humans using equipment to satisfy customers. The world is viewed as dynamic and complex and no engineer, no matter how smart, can anticipate in detail what will happen. The engineer's design is a ball park that serves as a starting point. People then make fine adjustments and improvements every day to learn the weaknesses of the system in order to strengthen it. The people doing the work have the best vantage to directly experience the complexities of the process and to identify its weaknesses. This produces and environment where it is safe to admit problems and get help to solve those problems. Through daily improvements (Kaizen), the system adjusts and adapts to changes in the environment and grows ever stronger. While in the mass production system the process is set to roll along as designed by the engineer and entropy inevitably sets in; with TPS, however, it is the people within the system that continually improve the system, making it better and better.

Dr. Shingo was a master of Kaizen. He had the scientific training and innovative genius to deeply understand processes and the humility to realize that he needed the operators to take ownership. I heard a great story about Dr. Shingo from a former executive of Kentucky Fried Chicken. They engaged Dr. Shingo as a consultant and at that point he was quite old, rolling into one of their restaurants in a wheel chair. He immediately wanted to see the entire operation and quickly determined it was a batch process based on push. It took a long time to cook the chicken so they prepared batches in advance and then heated them when they were ordered. That meant the chicken wasn't as fresh as it could have been and created undue waste. Dr. Shingo wanted to know why they did not cook to order; again they explained this was physically impossible given the time to cook the chicken. Dr. Shingo then sketched out a quick cook process that would allow them to cook to order. The executive's paradigm was instantly changed in that moment. He is now one of the top executives of one of the largest banks in the world and he immediately set to work applying TPS to banking. He had no hesitation about applying TPS to this very different type of process after learning the power of Kaizen and innovative thinking from Dr. Shingo.

In this book we learn how Dr. Shingo thinks about problems. You will not be overwhelmed by flowery prose and deep theoretical discussions in a Shingo book; what you will get is a straightforward methodology and examples to illustrate each concept. Those familiar with Toyota's practical problem solving will note the similarity perhaps because of the broad influence Shigeo Shingo had on TPS. You will learn about clearly defining the problem based on facts, questioning assumptions, the power of deep observation, using association to generate ideas, and overcoming resistance to new ideas. Those familiar with Toyota's thinking know that so much of the emphasis is on the up-front processes of properly defining the problem and thinking in terms of many alternatives. This is mostly the focus of this book and it is brought to life through real life examples of true innovation.

This book will help you understand the deep thinking that underlies the real practice of TPS. Many people seem more comfortable copying other people's "lean solutions." This is completely contrary to the spirit of TPS, which is actually about grasping the specific situation, thinking creatively, and constantly challenging your assumptions. We are fortunate to have this new opportunity to gaze deeply into the thinking of one of the true geniuses behind TPS—Dr. Shigeo Shingo.

Jeffrey K. Liker, Ph.D.
Professor, Industrial and Operations Engineering
The University of Michigan

A Note from the Publishers

Norman Bodek

We have a truly wonderful gift to share with you: a "new" book written by Dr. Shigeo Shingo in 1958. A few years back, I visited Mrs. Shingo in Fujisawa, Japan; it is something I have done every other year since Dr. Shingo's passing in 1990. On each of those visits I would look through Dr. Shingo's library hoping to find some past treasure to translate into English. When Mrs. Shingo showed me this book I had originally thought it to be too old to have translated. But, at the urging of my co-publisher, Collin McLoughlin, we both invested our time and efforts to bring this book to you. As you will see, Collin's intuition about this book was flawless, for this book is a masterpiece.

During the past seven years, I have been writing and teaching Quick and Easy Kaizen, a process that Toyota and other Japanese companies use to empower their employees in continuous improvement activities. Kaizen is a powerful process that can and will save the average company over $4000 per year, per employee, if applied. I simply urge organizations to ask their employees to begin to identify small problems in their own work area, find solutions, and then implement their improvement ideas on their own or with their work team. I ask people to make their work easier, more interesting, and to build their skills and capabilities. I request managers to simply ask their employees to come up with two implemented ideas per month. The result of this improvement activity is lower costs for the company, improved safety, improved quality, improved productivity, and much more involved and dedicated employees. *But until now, I did not teach people how to identify and solve the problems they detect.*

I unwittingly left people to their own devices on how to find and solve problems. Even though I had previously published many of Dr. Shingo's books, I did not realize that over 60 years ago he had developed a methodology called the *Scientific Thinking Mechanism* to find and eliminate problems.

After I published Dr. Shingo's *A Revolution in Manufacturing: The SMED System*, I received a telephone call from a consultant in Chicago thanking me for publishing the book. He said, "From the SMED book, I was able to help companies quickly reduce their change overs. Believe it or not Norman, I made a million dollars last year just by following Dr. Shingo's advice."

I am sure that many of you reading this book will also make a million dollars for your company by taking the material in this book and teaching the information to all of your employees.

As you read the book you will also see why Dr. Shingo is considered as one of the co-creators of the Toyota Production System and how his work has been a key in Toyota's financial success. Early on, Mr. Taiichi Ohno, vice president of Toyota, asked Dr. Shingo to teach Toyota engineers his problem solving techniques. He taught over 3000 Toyota employees.

Dr. Shingo was a master at finding and solving problems, but his greatest gift was his ability to teach others to do the same.

Collin McLoughlin

Without Dr. Shingo, the Toyota Production System would not be what it is today. In fact, a few years back Mr. Toyoda, former chairman of Toyota, was dedicating the opening of Toyota's first Chinese plant, and looked at Dr. Shingo's son, the president of Toyota China and said, "If it wasn't for Shingo's father Toyota would not be where they are today."

There has been much talk about the origins of the Toyota Production System and Dr. Shingo deserves significant credit for its creation. When you look at the life of Dr. Shingo and learn that he consulted with over 300 companies world-wide, such a debate becomes trivial. Yes, Toyota would not be the same without the benefit of Dr. Shingo's incredible mind, but if we look at the larger context of his life we see that Toyota is not the driving force behind his legacy. The fact that so many global companies entrusted their operations to his capable hands is Shigeo Shingo's true legacy.

This book has never been published in English; it is a newly discovered classic that will take its rightful place on every bookshelf along with Dr. Shingo's other great books. The book is designed to shake the foundation of the status quo. It will unveil the secret operational model that has never been seen in its entirety. Dr. Shingo's *Scientific Thinking Mechanism* is a proven model that has remained hidden for the last 50 years. Designed to systematically provide you with the method and structure to generate the ideas needed to get ahead and stay ahead. For brainstorming techniques, he teaches us how to stimulate the "silent area" of the brain where ideas are born. Most importantly, he instructs us to take objections to new ideas as advice, a powerful tool to be used when persuading people to accept improvements.

The analytical portions of this book rise above its technical nature due to Dr. Shingo's conversational writing style. His ability to illustrate points using humor and shop floor anecdotes will sharpen your mind as well as clarify your management approach. For the first time we have the principles, framework, and insight into the mind of the *original* Lean Manufacturing genius. For decades, Shigeo Shingo was the man to call to take a good company and turn it into a *great* company. His legacy and influence still guide us today; we only need to listen.

Norman once went to a Chinese restaurant where his fortune cookie said, "You have the ability to recognize the ability in others." How true! Norman's influence in the West is a direct reflection of the influence Dr. Shingo had on Norman. Their professional and personal relationship continues to have a profound and everlasting impact on industries around the globe.

Finally, we would like to thank the author, Dr. Shigeo Shingo, for his passion to improve the quality of life for everyone on the shop floor. By teaching us how to tear down the walls of the status quo, he demonstrates to us how to sharpen our minds to create and direct our own destiny.

Collin McLoughlin and Norman Bodek
Co-publishers

Acknowledgments

We would like to acknowledge the hard work of the following people: Satomi Umehara, for the precision of her translation from the original Japanese text; Tracy S. Epley, for his careful editing of the manuscript; and Khemanand Shiwram for design layout and his faithful reproduction of the original illustrations. We would also like to acknowledge our indebtedness to Mrs. Umeko Shingo, wife of Dr. Shingo, for discovering this book for us.

Collin McLoughlin and Norman Bodek
Co-publishers

I PRINCIPLES OF ANALYTICAL THINKING

> Science is defined as the systematic arrangement of knowledge. Systematic thinking and analysis is the key to successful problem solving and improvement.

The Edge of Night

A: What marks the boundary between day and night?

B: The setting of the sun, of course.

A: If that's the case, then why is it still light outside at sunset?

B: Well, how dark does it need to be? How about now, is this day or night?

A: This debate could go on all night. Why don't we simplify things and just call this ambiguous time period, "twilight"? Besides, it has a nice ring to it.

And so the conversation ends. Now, where do you draw the line between day and night?

1

Principle of Division

Let's assume that we are dividing the people in your department into different groups. First, we can divide them into male and female. Other possible classifications are:

1. Adult or youth

2. Business assistant or engineer

3. Those who are healthy or those who tend to be sick

Principle of Division Grouping Example	Table 1
Male or Female	Gender
Business Assistant or Engineer	Skills
Adult or child	Age
Healthy or Sick	Health Performance

The method used to create grouping criteria is called the "Principle of Division." When choosing criteria by which a group will be divided it is important to consider what kind and how many, divisions will be made. Furthermore, in order to prevent subsequent divisions from becoming vague or impossible, a "parent group" could be divided into a "grandparents and parents" group that is clearly distinct from one another, as in the manner of "A or not A."

Contrast and Continuation

I said to divide clearly, but there is a problem here. In the parent group there are "contrasting groups" which can be separated clearly, as in A or not A:

- Male or female

- Business assistant or engineer

And then there are "continuous groups" in which the distinction between two is not as easy to discern:

1. Adult and youth

2. Those who are healthy and those who tend to be sick

The Principles of Division governing the separation of continuous groups, such as age or health performance, are often hard to discern. As such, making a clear division in these groups can become difficult. In other words, dividing contrasting groups is easy, but dividing continuous groups often times is not.

At what age, do you think, does one transition from youth to adulthood? When the criteria for divisions are continuous like this we need to make a clear definition. For example, we could define those over 20 as adults. In terms of health performance, we would also need to make definitions, such as those based on healthy pulse, blood pressure, etc. However, it is somewhat odd to define someone who will turn 20 the following day as youth, and one who just turned 20 the previous day as adult.

As these examples illustrate, in the case of continuous groups it is essential for dividing criteria to be as clear and distinct as possible. However, even after assigning a definition it is possible for something to remain innately unclear. Therefore, if a parent group is a continuous group (such as distinguishing between 35 and 36 year old people), we should be fully aware of the difficulties that can arise when dividing it.

No Confusion, Yes?
Three brothers went to see their uncle in the country. He had two dogs.

Ichiro, being the oldest and tallest brother was the first to see them. "Look, the big dog and the little dog!" he said.

Jiro, who showed up later, said, "Oh, it's the red and white dogs."

The youngest brother, Saburo, heard his brothers' voices and came out of the house. "Oh boy! The white nosed dog and the black nosed dog," he said excitedly.

The confused dogs must have thought, "They are giving us

3

so many different names. What will we do if they call them all at once?"

Cross Division

A similar case could happen in a more familiar situation as well. Mr. Koga, who is in charge of material procurement, made four files related to the following:

1. Yawata Steel Works

2. Fuji Steel

3. Steel plate

4. Mold steel

Now, if you have an invoice of mold steel from Yawata, would you file it in number one or number four?

Trying to divide a parent group based on two different criteria is called "cross–division" and can often lead to confusion.

In the case of "the boundary between day and night," one source of confusion stems from the fact that two different division criteria, the time of sunset and the brightness of the sky, are imposed simultaneously. Another source of confusion originates from the inherent problems of brightness being a continuous group.* Consequently, the difficulties encountered when addressing this issue could be greatly reduced if the criterion for division is limited to brightness, and a clear boundary between day and night is defined. By categorizing our thoughts in this manner the question posed in the opening dialog could have been answered easily.

It is not uncommon for similar issues to pop up in daily conversation. For example, someone might say, "He is a stubborn capitalist, and an enemy of democracy!" This is a perfect example of cross–division.

---

*Astronomers have done this by classifying the intensity of light coming from distant stars.

4

What we need to compare to capitalism are other economic paradigms such as socialism, communism, and dictatorships that sit vis-à-vis democracy. There are of course other contrasting political ideas, such as internationalism versus nationalism.

When examining the differences between groups such as these it is crucial to acknowledge and properly evaluate the "gray area" that is likely to color the gap separating opposing views. Doing so can raise one's awareness for cross-divisional errors and help to minimize passing unfair judgment onto others during emotional discussions.

Perception is Reality

Reality is the man of twenty faces.* Let's assume that at Factory X the number of defects have steadily increased. In this case, things that should be taken into consideration are the following:

- If materials were satisfactory

- If processing methods were appropriate

- If inspections were done appropriately

- If handling of materials was proper

- If handling during transportation was appropriate

- If defects happened because materials were left unused for too long

Other things to take into account are:

- Components, hardness, strength, length, diameter, or surface roughness of the materials

- Processing machines, tools, workers' skills, and characteristics

---

*Fictitious criminal mastermind, Kaijin Niju Menso (The Mystery Man of Twenty Faces), nemesis of detective Akechi Kogoro whose exploits first appeared in an eponymous 1936 magazine serial in Japan.

- Lighting, noise, humidity, air quality, dust, temperature of the work area

- Methods of cutting, heat treatment, plating, and rust-removing

- Measuring devices for inspections, measuring environment, issues with inspectors

- The way products are placed, storage containers used, and the environment in which they are stored

- Packaging for transportation and types of transporting machines

- Whether the defect is in fact critical, considering the intended end–use of the product

This list demonstrates the extraordinary number of causes that could be contributing to the recent increase in defects. Things in reality have far more facets than we may realize. When faced with a problem like the one above we often attempt to solve them by simply focusing on a few causes we happen to put our finger on.

Things in reality are never that simple. They include:

- Many levels of divisions

- Continuous groups, and thus qualities inherently difficult to divide

- Numerous opportunities for cross–division, which inevitably leads to confusion

It is important to acknowledge the complexity of reality; it is comprised of a multitude of internal variables.

Bigger than a Breadbox?
When searching for the correct answer in question games such as "Who Am I?" or "Twenty Questions," having a good memory is helpful, but having the ability to apply analytical thinking skills

is far more effective.

Among principles of division, there are parent–child or "upper and lower" divisions, and sibling or "side to side" divisions. When playing the above–mentioned games, if you get stuck asking questions from upper to lower divisions, switch to a parallel line of questioning and you can often reach the answer much quicker.

An effective strategy for using these principles as analytical tools can be demonstrated in the following example of "Who am I?" Assuming the answer is Kinjiro Ninomiya*, note how the questions are grouped, divided, and ordered to provide the most efficient path for reaching the answer. Also, note the use of horizontal divisions when the child group of "Place" in Table 2b, is switched horizontally from Tokyo to Nagoya.

Who Am I Example	Table 2a
Gender	Male or Female
Existence	Imaginary or Real
Time Period	Past or Present

If the subject is in the past, what is an approximate time? (It is a continuous group, so you need to divide into different time frames.)

Nationality	Japanese or Not Table 2b
Place	East or West of Tokyo if Japan If not Japan, East or West of Nagoya
Job	Samurai, Merchant or Farmer
Status	Feudal Lord or Regular Samurai
Accomplishments	War, Financial Reconstruction, Forestation, Flood Control, etc.

*Kinjiro Ninomiya was a prominent 19th century agricultural leader, philosopher, moralist, and economist.

If you go through these divisions in proper order, getting to the right answer is not difficult. In reality you might be given some of the hints beforehand, so it might even be easier.

The same principle can be applied to "Twenty Questions." In this case, divisions like the following should be added:

Life Form	Plant, Animal, Mineral	Table 2c
Dimensions	Size, Length	
Shape	Circle, Square, Undefined	
Number	Group or Individual	
Price	Approximate Value	
Ownership	Public or Private	
Movement	Mobile or Stationary	
Sense	Sight, Touch, Smell, Hearing, Taste	

Thinking in Two

The most advanced electronic statistical machine is supposed to divide in geometric progressions of two:

Divide A into A1 and A2

Divide A1 into A1-1 and A1-2

Divide A2 into A2-1 and A2-2

You can keep on dividing infinitely in this manner. Thinking in terms of two like this is the easiest method of division for humans. Nevertheless, we should be cautious not to fall into the trap of polarized thinking. We all have unconscious assumptions like the following:

Things that are not good are bad

Things that are not bad are good

We also have unconscious definitions that establish our concept of:

- Approval and denial

- Good and evil

- Long and short

8

Parent and child, husband and wife, brother and sister— we tend to think in terms of two and often in polarized, fixed confrontation. But we should not restrict the natural flexibility of our mind as it tries to expand infinitely beyond that boundary. For within these divisions there are always other things that can be divided, and even still more after that, and everywhere in between. As long as we are aware of this nature of constant divisions, thinking in terms of two will be a powerful solution when trying to elucidate the mystery of reality.

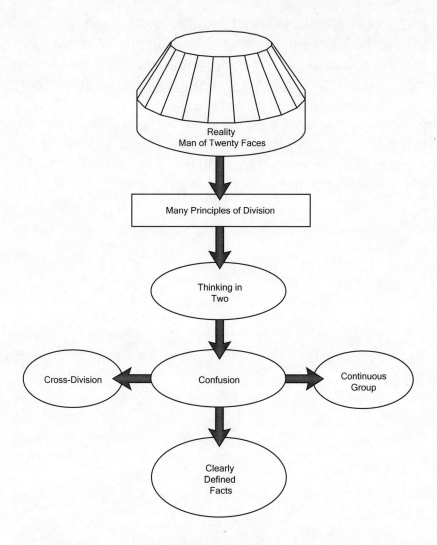

Figure 1 Reality Tree

The "Man of Twenty Faces" is a metaphor reflecting how perception defines reality and no two eyes see the same details. To get to the truth of the matter, critical analysis is needed to comprehend the entire issue in order to arrive at clearly defined facts.

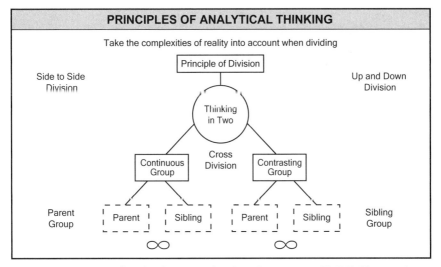

Figure 2 Scientific Thinking Mechanism Component (STM) Chapter 1

Being aware of the complexitites of reality is the first step and the Principle of Division's strength lies in its ability to reduce those complexities to managable elements. The ability to think in terms of two will provide the relative criteria grouping. Contrasting groups (man or woman, war or peace), and continuous groups (adult or youth, healthy or sick), may contain subdivisional groups which can be divided indefinitely. The ability to categorize criteria during the creative process is where this model sources its power for the individual.

II CAPTURING PROBLEMS

> Improvement, the act of bettering things beyond their current status, can only occur after one has captured and understood the full nature of a current problem.

There are three essential steps to problem solving:

- Find the problem
- Clarify the problem
- Find the cause

This chapter will identify and explain each step.

Finding Problems

Everyday we face problems that need to be solved and situations that need to improve. Nevertheless, there are many occasions when we do not even realize a problem exists, or we misunderstand the nature of the problem altogether.

Never Accept the Status Quo

Problems that need to be addressed often do not emerge as problems unless people are inquisitive enough to question the norm.

People who live in the city may think the sun rises from the roofs. Whereas, those who live by the sea may believe it rises from the water; those in the mountains may even believe that it comes up from out of the snow covered peaks.

Many people in Japan who have spent long hours standing in rush-hour buses and trains probably never questioned if there was an alternative way to commute. And yet, I have heard that in France, buses often pass stops if there are no seats left to sit down, and customers do not try to force themselves into crowded buses. This made me wonder why in Japan, there are people sitting comfortably and people standing for long periods of time, but both pay exactly the same price for transportation. In other words, a question and a problem arose in my mind.

We need to be aware of problems and be passionate about being dissatisfied with the status quo; more importantly, we need to bond that dissatisfaction with our desire to improve.

Those who are always satisfied with the current situation and do not question it will never be able to see problems; the status quo is a comfort to them. On the other hand, those who do question will find that, not only can they see the problem, but the very act of asking will lead them halfway to a solution.*

At one press shop I went to, rectangular parts were being punched out of large plastic sheets. While I was there, I saw the leftover boards from which the parts were made.

"The spacing between parts seems rather large. Is there any reason for this?" I asked the supervisor.

"Well, I wanted to make them smaller, but the rounded edges make it difficult."

---

*Editor's emphasis

"Do the edges need to be round?"

"Well, we just do the manufacturing here so I don't really know."

After this conversation I went to the assembly plant to see how these parts were actually used. There I found out that the parts were used as electric insulators in places where they cannot be seen from the outside. Thus, the shape of the edges was not important.

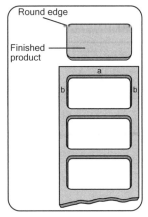

Figure 3 Part Stamping

The press shop changed the design accordingly. As a result the spaces between the parts and the spaces on the sides of the board were eliminated, boosting their yield by 30 percent.

If the shop supervisors had asked questions such as "Why is there so much wasted material?" or "Do the parts really need round edges?" the problem could have been identified and solved much sooner.

We all become accustomed to our surroundings. Often, we become complacent about the way things are and cease to be dissatisfied about them. Asking ourselves questions such as "Are there any problems that need to be addressed?" or "Is there anything that could be improved?" even once a day, is a conscious exercise we could all benefit from practicing.

The Magnitude of the Unknown

G Industries has a factory that produces plywood. In plywood production maintaining a high yield is essential since it directly affects the product price.

It was in this factory that I once had the chance to observe the log peeling process. The log is peeled into sheets of veneer as it rotates on a lathe. Centering and mounting the log correctly determines how much veneer can be produced and, correspondingly, how high the yield will be. The technical aspect of mounting the log for maximum yield was done by experienced workers. Here is how they determined the center of the log:

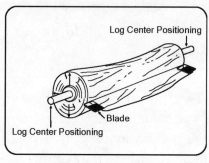

Figure 4 Log Axis

- Measure the widest diameter and shortest diameter of the log and calculate the center
- Adjust the center depending on the curve of the log
- Press the log into the machine to lock it in the center axis of rotation

As a technician was about to start peeling, I began to wonder if the axis was really accurate. I asked him to stop and performed the following measurements:

- Divide the circumference of the end of the log by eight
- Divide the length by six

Extend the eight points of the circumference lengthwise down the log intersecting with the six cross sections, and use the resulting points to calculate six centers which can then be averaged to provide an overall center for the log.

As a result of this more accurate measurement, it became clear that the original measurement was in error by as much as 20 mm. Using an erroneous axis of rotation will produce a discontinuous veneer that is unfit for first–grade material. Furthermore, as the following calculations show, the error occurs at a critical area where the circumference is the largest, greatly compromising the potential yield.

Conventional measuring: $\pi/4 (410-150)2 - \pi/4 (260)2 = 100\%$

New accurate measuring: $\pi/4 (410-150)2 = \pi/4 (300)2 = 134\%$

Indeed, 34 percent of the yield had been wasted with the conventional measuring method. As a result of this finding the new measuring method was adopted immediately.

The above example provides a good illustration of the magnitude of an unknown problem and how it remains unknown until questions are asked.

Since experienced workers were in charge of calculating the center axis, the factory had simply trusted the conventional method of finding the center axis. Even though 34 percent of the wood had been wasted, no one actually knew if the method was appropriate or not. Until someone questioned the conventional method, vast amounts of material and resources had been wasted.

Here is another story. M Industries keeps books when materials are purchased. An accountant told me about a problem with this system:

"The book (cost) method is inconvenient when it comes to cost accounting."

So, I suggested switching to the invoice (sales) method, but the accountant opposed.

"We can't do that."

"Why not?"

"It would be a problem if invoices go missing."

"So, how is it going to be a problem if that happens?"

"Well, you know… it's just going to be a problem."

"How so?"

The accountant was struggling to provide an answer to his own vague scenario. We both grew uncomfortable as he sought his mind for words, so I offered him these possibilities, "I guess it would be a problem for two reasons: number one, how do you know if invoices go missing, and number two, how do you recover the content of a missing invoice?"

"Exactly!" the relieved accountant exclaimed.

"The first problem can be solved by writing sequential numbers on the invoices. That way when they come back, you can just check to see if any numbers are missing. The second problem can be resolved by making a copy. Regardless, it should be an infrequent problem, if it happens at all."

So, the invoice method was introduced at the company and no major confusion ensued. As a result, the cost accounting became much more streamlined.

Again, this example highlights the needless setbacks that can occur by being comfortable with what we know. True, the accountant knew it was going to be a problem *if* invoices went missing, but *why* it was going to be a problem was not clear.

When we try to solve problems, we need to ask the following questions first:

1. What do we know?
2. What don't we know?

The biggest obstacle in finding problems and improving the current situation is the blind belief that we know everything and that nothing needs to be changed. Even on issues that we think we have a good understanding of, asking the above questions will help us root out overlooked issues and set us on the path of improvement by clarifying the unknown and, ultimately, solving our problems.

We Act on What We Think is "True"
As humans, we usually base our decisions and actions on what we perceive to be true, as opposed to what actually is.

Don't Act on Assumptions
All too often we conclude that "telling what we know first-hand" and "telling what we heard from someone else" are equally valid.

For example, "I saw termites in the bathroom pillars" conveys what you know first-hand. On the other hand, saying, "Mr. Takemoto told me that termites are in the bathroom pillars," relates only what you have heard.

The former is based on fact, whereas the latter requires us to make an assumption of fact.

When I go to a factory and ask how their process improvement is going, a foreman might say, "I think our production scheduling is reasonable. The schedule coordinator should be having a meeting everyday and keeping it under control."

This makes me wonder why they even asked me to examine their process management in the first place; especially when I go to the factory floor and see that there are many work-in-process goods, as well as parts in stock—typical signs of process mismanagement.

However, when I talk with the coordinator he might say, "We haven't had a standard production schedule recently because creating one is so time consuming," or "I know we should be having a meeting everyday, but I'm busy taking care of invoices for the factory. I don't have much time to do anything else; as a matter of fact, there hasn't been a meeting for six months or so."

Thus, the foreman's reply was based on the "imaginary truth" that things were going well. The reality of the factory however, showed otherwise.

When people act based on notions which they believe to be true, improvements take a back seat and problems take the wheel. I once heard someone say, "People don't want to constantly expend the energy it takes to find out what is true for themselves, so they often rely on what they hear without confirming whether it's accurate or not."

The result of the next experiment backs up this saying. Below is the breakdown of people's reactions when they were asked what they did not know.

Answers When Faced with Lack of Knowledge		Table 3
Answer based on guessing		62%
	(Maybe	23%)
	(Must be	39%)
Answer with "I don't know"		35%
No answer		3%

This shows that when people are asked what they do not know, six out of ten people answer with guesswork, and among those six, four would answer with assertion and basically end up lying.

Their lies are not intentional, and come out almost subconsciously. Yet, this makes their type of response all the more troublesome. This is especially the case when the things said are shown to be untrue and we try to lie ourselves out of the lies.

Trying to find problems based on either a hunch or a guess entails risk. When we are trying to discern problems it is important to base our judgment on factual truth.

We sometimes hear conversations like the following during meetings:

"I heard that this happened."

"I don't think it did."

If both sides do not know the truth it ends up being a he-said–she-said type of argument. We need to keep in mind that diagnosing problems is oftentimes a constant process of separating what is true from what seems to be true.

Things Change as Time Goes By
One evening Dr. Tanaka got a phone call in the middle of the night. It was from Riku, who lives on a farm about 30 minutes away.

"Hello, Doctor. I know it's very late, but I was wondering if you could come to my house."

"What happened?"

Dr. Tanaka, whose sleep was disrupted, was not in the best of moods.

"Well, my wife is sick."

"Tell me more about her condition."

"She says her lower abdomen hurts. We suspect that it's appendicitis."

"Appendicitis? That can't be Riku; I removed her appendix last spring. Don't you remember?" The doctor sounded like he was about to hang up.

Figure 5 Things Change as Time Goes By

"Wait, wait . . . it was actually my ex-wife that you operated on. It is my new wife who is sick now."

If we don't think about the passage of time, confusion and trouble are bound to happen as this anecdote humorously warns us.

At R stationery factory, there was a process which called for products to be dried. While other processes only took twelve minutes, drying took 40 and created a major bottleneck.

Temperature, humidity, and air flow are three main factors that influence drying. I went to the shop floor and saw that egg incubators were being used for this process. However, the incubators had only small outlets for ventilation, and therefore had very limited air flow. I immediately saw the shortcomings of this method and went to find a hair dryer, just like the type that you would see at a hair salon.

I put the products in a box and dried them with the hair dryer. The result of the experiment was this: drying time was reduced to about 13 minutes, one third of what it was before. Moreover, this process no longer delayed the whole assembly process.

I was later told that the previous material, made from celluloid, required a curing process (heating the material at a certain temperature for a while to stabilize it) so the introduction of incubators was actually appropriate. However, after adopting a new material and switching to drying instead of curing, they continued to use the same method without putting much thought into it.

At another factory I went to, I suggested using sintered alloy for a part they were manufacturing. The head of the manufacturing department immediately opposed.

"No, we can't do that."

"Why not?"

"Because the cost is prohibitive."

"Do you know how much it costs?"

"Doesn't it cost around $20 per pound?"

"No, you can get it for about $7 per pound."

"Is that so?"

"Why did you think it was so expensive?"

"Well, because I checked the price before, and it was extremely high."

"I see."

"Actually, this was about three years ago. I didn't know that the price has changed so much."

As these examples illustrate, we can easily overlook problems if we do not realize that things change as time goes by. When addressing problems we need to keep in mind that neither the past, nor the future, is written in stone.

Love is Blind

It is sometimes said, "Love is blind." For a person in love, oftentimes it is the only thing that matters in life and they cannot see anything else. On the same parallel, we occasionally fall prey to other forms of "blindness" within our minds.

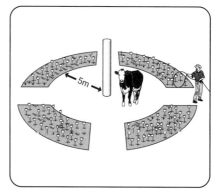

In a magazine that came out around 1935, there was a quiz:

A cow escaped from its pasture and ran towards a pristine flower bed. A cowboy rushed after and managed to capture it. The flower bed was arranged

Figure 6 Mental Blindspot

in a circular fashion with a pole in the middle of it. The cowboy had a rope which was 2 meters long, so he tied it to the cow.

The pole was about 5 meters away from the flower beds. Concluding that the cow would not be able to reach the beds, he left to seek help. When he returned with some extra hands, however, the flower beds were destroyed.

What do you think had happened there?

The answer? — Nothing was said about tying the rope to the pole. Though it is a silly question, it does point out a "blind spot" in people's minds — in this case, upon hearing that a 2 meter rope was tied to the cow, we have a tendency to jump to the conclusion that the rope was also tied to the pole.

Mastering the Obvious

Let's look at the next question. Can you answer how many squares there are in figure 7? Many people would not think to hard about it and quickly answer, 16.

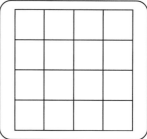

Figure 7 Sixteen Squares?

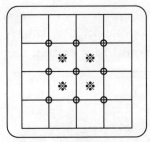

Figure 8 Thirty Squares

Others would take their time and realize that there is the big outer square and say, 17.

The correct answer is 30, as illustrated, in figure 8 and Table 4.

This is another example of a mental blind spot; there are things we see, yet still do not comprehend their existence.

Thinking In & Out of the Box	Table 4
The biggest square	1
9 – block square (✖ as the center)	4
4 – block square (o as the center)	9
1 – block square	16
	Total 30

I once inspected Mitsubishi's shipyard in Nagasaki not long after the local bus line had been extended to Tategami, at the end of the factory. Up until then people had to use the municipal ferry to get to the area, so this was a big improvement.

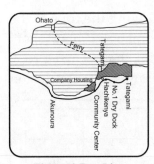

Figure 9 Bus Line

There were new bus stops in the following order from Akunoura, the previous terminal of the line: Akunoura, Community Center, Dry Dock #1, and Tategami. There is an entrance to the outfitting yard in an area called Hachikenya, between the community center and Dry Dock #1. In the morning, I would see many people get off the bus at the community center and rush toward Hachikenya to go to work.

Then I thought to myself, "If there was a stop at Hachikenya, it would be more convenient. But the community center is close to company housing, so maybe many people use it. Besides, the distance between the stops would be too close."

24

About 15 days after the bus line was extended however, a new bus stop sign, Hachikenya, appeared and the buses started to stop there. Only then did I realize my own mental blind spot—thinking that the stops would be too close. I forgot that a bus company's top service priority is the convenience of customers.

The figure at the right is the top view of an object. The figure below it is the front view of the same object. Can you guess what the side view looks like?

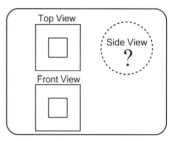

Figure 10 Process Within a Process

What confuses everyone is the little square in the middle, if it were a hole that went through, the lines would be dotted. Then we realize that for the little square to be in the middle of both views the big square must be the slope of a triangular box.

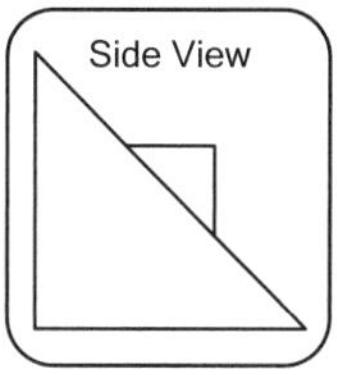

An illustration of such an object is shown in Figure 11. Note that the protrusion in the middle could be an indentation instead.

Figure 11 Depicting Setup

The difficulty of the question arises from the preconception that we are looking at something square with a square hole on it. Looking at it without any sort of assumptions will make it easier to find an answer.

During World War II in England, a mother and a daughter were stranded in the countryside after their car ran out of gas. Gasoline was expensive, and even if they had a rationing ticket, they would have had to go home to get it. As it got darker, the 15-year-old daughter hit upon an idea:

"Mom, do you think the car will run on alcohol?"

They went to the store and bought a bottle of strong alcohol and to their surprise, the engine started.

25

We all have the preconception that cars can only function with gasoline, but they will work as long as fuel applicable for internal combustion is used, although the efficiency will vary.

These examples point to us the trap of preconceptions in our thinking. When we believe that there is no problem, we have to question if the belief is built on false assumptions.

Furthermore, if we could describe a problem with words, record it, or picture it, that will help us capture more problems. If we ask ourselves questions such as "What don't we know?", "What do we know?", and "What are we looking for?" they will allow us to have a firmer grasp on problems.

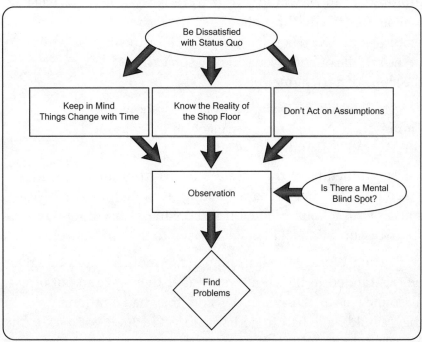

Figure 12 Clarifying Problems

Clarifying Problems
Even if a problem is discovered, a solution will not follow unless the nature of the problem is clarified.

Ambiguous Descriptions

Why is job shop lead time excessive?

I had the following conversation while visiting a machine tool maker:

"The production period seems a bit long. Do you have any ideas on how we can shorten it?"

"How long is it now?"

"About ten months, I think we can cut it down some."

The department chiefs who were nearby also put their two cents in.

"We could probably shorten it by half a month."

"I think even a month would be possible."

Then I asked them, "When you say ten months what aspect of production are you referring to?"

"The ten months encompasses design, manufacturing, assembly, and test operation."

Production Timeline Breakdown	Table 5
Design	4 months
Manufacturing	3 months
Assembly	2 months
Test Operation	1 month

Some other ambiguous reasons contributing to the excessive production time were also provided: "We sometimes outsource our part manufacturing"; "Test operations can often be tedious due to improper design, materials, or processing." One simply said, "The design period is too long."

Such vague descriptions of the problem will never foster the formulation of a solution. Instead, we must think analytically and ask questions such as the following:

- Is the basic design taking a long time?

27

- Are negotiations with the client on specifications taking too long?

- If the above is the case, is the delay regarding functionality or structure?

- If it is structure, what part of the structure is it?

Approaching problems in this chronological manner will help eliminate ambiguity. Yet, all too often when I visit a factory specializing in individual manufacturing (a job shop), people offer comments that fail to capture the crux of the problem.

As if they had already given up on improvement a foreman might say, "We just do individual manufacturing here so there isn't much we can change." This is not the case at all. Although there is not much leeway in what they manufacture there is certainly room for improvement on how they manufacture.

Take ship building for example. Typically, ships are built on the basis of individual orders. However, 60% of the part manufacturing consists of marking and flame cutting. The rest involves machine pressing, roller bending, and heat bending. Therefore, if the focus is placed on the production method as opposed to the product itself, the flow production system, usually reserved for mass-production, can be just as applicable in ship building.

I was once told that setting a standard time for the process of bending plates for the hull is impossible, since the size of the plates and degree of bend will vary from one ship to the next. I suggested setting a range of standard times for each task depending on plate size, degree of bend, and the thickness of plates. Later, they implemented this idea successfully.

Clearly, just saying "we can't change because we do individual production here," or "we can't do it because there are many types of plates," would be a short–sighted and inaccurate conclusion. As the above examples demonstrate, by analyzing its elementary components we both clarify a problem and simultaneously gain insight regarding its solution.

Five Elements of Problems

One basic categorization method used for analyzing problems is called the "5Ws & 1H":

5Ws & 1H	Table 6
Who? (subject)	
What? (object)	
When? (time)	
Where? (space)	
Why? (purpose)	
How? (method)	

When a problem is identified, it is helpful to subdivide it into elements of "who, what, when, where, why and how?" Many of these elements can even be divided again, sometimes infinitely. For instance, consider the following "what" (Object) questions in this example involving machine tools.

"What part of the machine tool? What stage of the machine tool production–design, part manufacturing, assembly, or test operations? Can part manufacturing be divided into those produced in house and those that are outsourced? If it is outsourced, further divisions can be made concerning part type, region, and quantity of order.

Note that the question "why" can be directed to each of the elemental categories above it, such as "Why is (object) a problem?" or "Why does this person (subject) do a certain task?" As such, "why" by itself, does not constitute a fundamental element of a problem. Though it is a useful tool in the discovery of what these elements might be.

It should be noted that the designation of object (for "what" questions) and subject (for "who" questions) could be used as an alternative label for these elements in certain situations. For example, a machine tool is considered to be the "what" at a machine tool factory, yet it would be considered the "who" at an auto factory.

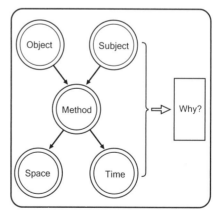

Figure 13 Five Elements of Problems

We could think about the same concept in terms of a company trip. In this example, the "what" are the people going on the trip, while the "who" is the vehicle that transports them such as a bus, train, ship, etc. This can be somewhat counter-intuitive. In cases like the one above, using the terms "object" or "subject," instead of using "what" and "who" will help reduce confusion.

Consider the following problem at a factory: The number of suggestions for improvement seems to be dropping recently.

Improving Improvement Ideas	Table 7
Object:	What kind of suggestions, work method, safety, work environment, management, etc.?
Subject:	Who comes up with suggestions, engineers, foreman, manager, etc.?
Method:	Is the number of suggestions decreasing due to the lack of ideas? Is it due to complicated procedures? Is it because creating product drawings takes time? Is there a problem with the evaluation method? Is there a problem associated with rewards? Are people concerned about others' criticism?
Space:	Where do people bring up ideas, factory floor, or office; is there a suggestion box in the office? Where is the box placed?
Time:	When do people suggest ideas? Always, on certain days, once a month, twice a month, etc.? When are the ideas discussed? When do people decide if the ideas will be adopted or not?

Asking these questions will clarify problems and lead us to the appropriate solutions.

Two Streams of Production

As stated in the beginning of this section, there are five elements which constitute problems. In reality however, these elements are interwoven in a fluid and dynamic network composed entirely of object and subject (Figure 14): The flow of objects moves in one direction, converging with the flow of subjects from the other. Overall flow from these two streams is affected by changes in the other three elements: method, space, and time.*

Machines and tools assist workers so they are included as subjects. Therefore, how machines change in the flow of space and time must be taken into account.

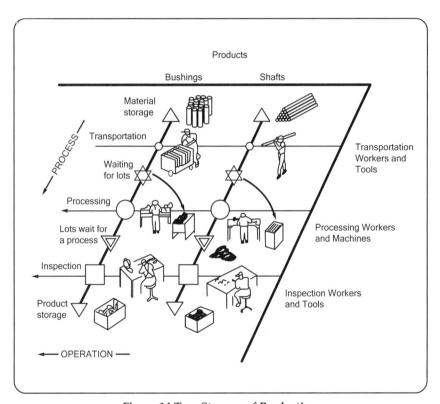

Figure 14 Two Streams of Production

---

*Dr. Shingo starts to make a clear distinction between operations, individual production machines, and the overall process flow. Prior to this discovery, almost all manufacturing companies optimized each machine center to produce more and more inventory and huge buffers of inventory would clog the factory floors. It was this spark of recognition that gave birth to the Toyota Production System.

Manufacturing Flow	Table 8
Flow of Objects	Flow of items (Processes)
Flow of Subjects	Flow of people (Operations)

The flow of objects is called "processes" in manufacturing and consists of the following four main components:

Object Flow	Table 9
Processing (only Value Added component)	Altering form and/or quality, assembly, disassembly
Inspection	Comparison with standards
Transportation	Change in position
Delay	No activities, only time changes

Among these four components only processing adds value to products. Inspection simply assures whether or not processing is done correctly, and is therefore considered a passive activity.

Transportation occurs as many times as actual processing steps. However, such a process only contributes to raising the price of products. For this reason, eliminating transportation is an integral part of factory improvement. To accomplish this, improving layout of the plant is the first thing to consider. Improving the method of transportation itself only comes next. Buffers are designed to work as delays against unstable production. If we reconsider this premise, they can usually be halved. Each of these four processes marks a point of intersection with the flow of subjects, called "operations," which can be divided into the following three activities:

Operations Flow	Table 10
Principle Operations	Main and Incidental Operations
Margin Allowances	Allowances for fatigue, physical and operational necessity, and unexpected incidents
Preparation and Clean-Up	Preparation before work, cleanup after work

Preparation, Clean–Up

Preparing for work and cleaning up after work; also called set–up changeover.

Actual Operations

Primary operation:

Actual grinding (processing)

Measuring (inspection)

Loading product (transportation)

Placing in warehouse (storage)

Associated operation:

Mount product on machine for grinding (processing)

Measuring (inspection)

Loading product (transportation)

Placing in warehouse (storage)

Margin Allowances

Fatigue allowance: taking a rest during work

Hygiene allowance: restroom breaks, drinking water

Operations allowance: lubricating machines, etc.

Workplace Allowance: halting work due to material shortage, machinery failure, etc.

Among these different types of work, only the main operation is the actual work that increases value. By improving incidental operations, preparation, cleanup, or various margins, work efficiency can be boosted tremendously.

This idea of two streams of production can easily be applied to phenomena outside of factories, as demonstrated by the following reanalysis of our company trip example. Assume that your task is to take employees to the destination.

- Object: 50 employees participating in the trip

33

- Subject: bus (driver) or train (conductor)

Processes of the trip can be compared to the four components of production processes as follows:

1. Taking employees to the destination: transportation

2. Waiting for a bus or train: delay

3. Checking to see that no one is missing: inspection

4. Playing sports or having lunch: processing

Assuming transportation is by bus, the breakdown of "operations" components would be:

- Preparation: inspection and maintenance before the trip

- Primary operation: driving

- Associated operation: loading and unloading people

- Leeway for fatigue: taking a break from driving

- Leeway for physical necessity: taking restroom stops

- Leeway for operational necessity: stopping the bus to adjust the rearview mirror

- Leeway for unexpected matters: getting stuck in traffic

As we can now see, every phenomenon is made up of the aforementioned five elements: object, subject, method, space, and time. All of these elements directly contribute to the streams of production, consisting of the flow of objects, or processes, and the flow of subjects, or operations. Perceiving the structure of everyday phenomena in this manner is a powerful cognitive tool that can be used to effectively elucidate any problem we encounter.

Gilbreth's 18 Therbligs

In the Japanese writing system, the character (*kanji*) for work can be divided into two parts, respectively meaning person, and move. Indeed, there is a tendency to think that when people are in motion they are working. However, this is not always true

Taking another look, the same kanji could be divided into three parts:

Person + Weight + Strength

Figure 15 Kanji for Work

This is a more accurate meaning of work: "a person exerting strength on a weighty task." In other words we should not assume that just because a man is in motion that he is working. Rather, we should confirm that he is exerting his strength in a productive way. In the context of manufacturing this is precisely the sort of action that should be maximized in the movement of our personnel. To accomplish this, we must first establish a means of analyzing movement and assessing how it contributes to overall productivity. One such system was created by Frank B. Gilbreth.

According to Gilbreth's research all human movements can be reduced to basic elements. At the abstract level these motions are repeated from the cradle to the grave. Gilbreth called these elemental motions therbligs* and organized them with respect to manufacturing into those that add value and those that are wasteful. Note in Figure 16 on the following page that only the elements of Assemble, Disassemble, and Use are truly beneficial; all other elements are mere "movements of the body," and as such are void of productive value and should be minimized as much as possible. Gilbreth was not concerned with Time Study

---

* "Therblig" is a play on word of Gilbreth; it is Gilbreth spelled backwards with the 'th' transposed. Like Dr. Shingo and his Single Minute Exchange of Die, Frank Gilbreth created a timesaving method for bricklaying that is still in use today. As a testament to the scientific nature of Gilbreth's system, therblig studies are still used today in fields ranging from process improvement to robotics.

and never assigned times for each of his basic elements of motion; he was interested only in eliminating unnecessary movements and believed the shortest cycle time would follow.

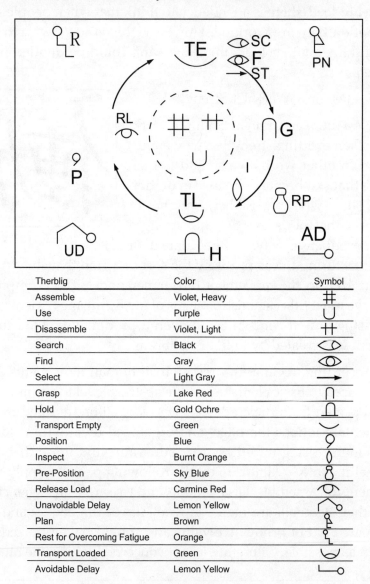

Therblig	Color	Symbol
Assemble	Violet, Heavy	⊞
Use	Purple	U
Disassemble	Violet, Light	╫
Search	Black	⌖
Find	Gray	⊙
Select	Light Gray	→
Grasp	Lake Red	∩
Hold	Gold Ochre	∩
Transport Empty	Green	‿
Position	Blue	♀
Inspect	Burnt Orange	◊
Pre-Position	Sky Blue	8
Release Load	Carmine Red	⌒
Unavoidable Delay	Lemon Yellow	⌂o
Plan	Brown	♟
Rest for Overcoming Fatigue	Orange	⌇
Transport Loaded	Green	⌣
Avoidable Delay	Lemon Yellow	L—o

Figure 16 Eighteen Therbligs

Viewing human motion in this manner is an effective way to capture problems. As mentioned earlier, the five elements of problems are object, subject, space, time, and method. Furthermore, since tools and machines also contribute to method, therbligs apply to them as well.

What's the Topic Again?

During lunch break one of the workers, Mr. K, struck up a conversation:

"I've heard that highball's are a good drink for women, but not for men."

"Why's that? It seems like an alright drink for a guy to have," contended another.

Others joined and the argument went on. Then, someone asked, "What aspect of the drink is bad?"

Mr. K replied, "I've heard that using a carbonated beverage to dilute whiskey has a negative effect on men's virility."

The other men needed no further convincing and the argument ended there.

As demonstrated in this example, we often carry a conversation without ever clarifying what the subject or topic really is. Take the commonly used phrase, "Let's go." It is completely unclear as to whom, what, or where it refers. In daily conversation this is usually not an issue. A coworker might say, "Let's go have another drink," and the other person usually understands what it means.

During work however, this kind of ambiguity can be hazardous. Therefore, it is extremely important to communicate with clear and complete sentences.

Losing Sight of the Forest

As I mentioned earlier, speaking about problems too generally or ambiguously will not lead to solutions. Yet, just seeing one aspect of the issue without seeing the whole picture is also a trap that can be hard to avoid.

Nature's Call

In a large working environment such as a shipyard, it is no surprise that restroom issues sometimes arise.

Workers at a shipyard once told management that there should be more toilets (at this time there was no such thing as a "port-o-potty" and workers took care of business using a bucket). A few days later, the person in charge of this issue said he took care of the problem.

However, complaints still came rolling in. So management decided to look into what had really been done. It turned out that the measures taken were poorly thought out and left much room for improvement:

Buckets without proper lids were used and they were few and far between.

The person in charge changed frequently and, correspondingly, so did the manner in which this issue was dealt with.

Buckets were placed in areas that were too exposed.

Buckets were taken away after hours.

The person in charge of the toilets thought that just placing more buckets around the yard would be sufficient. But this was not the case at all. Since he neglected to consider other factors — if workers could use them comfortably and conveniently, for example — the issue remained unsolved.

As this example illustrates, we can not fix problems by having a narrow focus on just one aspect of a situation; we must step back to take a look at the bigger picture. Doing so will allow us to see as many of the causes as possible.

Small Foundry Floor Space

I once visited a foundry in Yamaguchi prefecture which produced steel wheels for coal carts.

"Orders have recently increased and we're running out of floor space. I'm thinking about buying the building next door, but their asking price is ridiculous. I'm not sure what to do," said the plant manager.

The foundry was about 400 square meters with hundreds of casting molds spread across the floor. Workers were busy ladling molten iron from the furnace to each mold.

I asked the manager, "Why are there so many molds on the floor?"

"Why? Well, because we have to make so many wheels each day."

"Yes of course, I understand that. But just because you have to create 300 wheels doesn't mean that you need to have 300 molds on the floor at once."

"What are you saying?"

"Well, let me see if I have your production steps right. First, you make the molds, and then pour the molten iron. Then you must wait for the iron to cool and solidify before you can take the product out. Once taken out, you have to remove any sharp edges and deburr the casting. Finally, you have to treat the sand for re-use.

"Currently, the interval between mold making and iron pouring is very large. Because of this you consume a great deal of floor space with molds to maximize production. However, if you were to eliminate that interval and make the process more repetitive, you wouldn't need all these molds waiting on the floor at once.

"In fact, many foundries have introduced conveyors to do just that. I'm not saying that a conveyor's a must, but it's worth looking into. As long as you can completely perform a production cycle 300 times a day, you can make 300 products. So really, the size of this plant isn't an issue at all."

The manager replied, "I've never looked at it like that before. I'll look into what it would take to introduce a conveyor system here."

Up until this point, because the manager's solution only considered floor space, he ignored other more reasonable options without even realizing it. This example emphasizes the importance of taking into account all the five elements — object, subject, method, space, and time — when faced with problems.

Checklist Approach

Another effective way to analyze a problem is by listing its characteristics and the corresponding flaws associated with them.

Take a picture frame as an example.

Possible Characteristics:

A. shape — square, circle, oval, triangle, three-dimensional, multi-faceted

B. covers — glass, plastic, nothing

C. frame — wood, aluminum, plastic, no frame

D. how pictures are inserted — from the back, side, or top

E. how frames are mounted — wire hook, suction cup, magnet

F. frame color — different colors, patterns

Let us think about the possible flaws associated with each characteristic:

- the frame accommodates only one size print
- the top and bottom are indistinguishable
- the glass is too shiny

- the frame is too heavy

- changing pictures is tedious

- pictures slip easily

- imbalanced once it is hung

- the hanging mechanism is obtrusive

- paint on the frame comes off easily

- the back collects too much dust

- hanging is unidirectional

- it is too expensive

Sometimes, making a checklist of characteristics can be a useful method for analyzing a problem. For example:

| Checklist | | | Table 11 |
Characteristics			
Length	Width	Thickness	Height
Depth	Weight	Firmness	Size
Volume	Angle	Strength	Slipperiness
Viscosity	Density	Number	Time
Speed	Wattage	Temperature	Humidity
Ventilation	Cost	Price	Quality
Frequency of use	Taste	Smell	Odor
Sound	Half-life	Efficiency	Color

Characteristics on checklists will vary depending on the problem. The purpose however, is always the same: make clear what is known, what is unknown, and what needs to be known. This approach will ensure a solid understanding of any problem.

Qualitative and Quantitative Knowledge

"Numbers stimulate the brain," an expression goes. This demonstrates the importance of analyzing things quantitatively with numbers. From my experience, I believe this concept to be true and very effective in many aspects of plant improvement.

An ore analysis produced the following two results which highlight the difference between qualitative and quantitative analysis:

Qualitative analysis—"It contains copper, gold, lead, and sulfur."

Quantitative analysis—"It has 5 percent of copper, 0.5 percent of gold, 8 % of lead, and 3 percent of sulfur."

When we think we "know" things, either we might know them qualitatively or we might know them quantitatively, and how we know actually changes the way we act.

Quantitative Savings

When I visited T factory, many machines were idle.

"Why aren't they operating?" I asked.

The factory manager said, "The cutting blades are being sharpened."

"It looks like that's affecting a lot of machines. Why don't you introduce a central sharpening system?"

"Well, sometimes the machines are offline because of it, but I don't think it's much of a problem here. After all, this isn't a big factory. A central sharpening system would seem excessive."

At the end of our conversation, he said he needed to rush to the bank to arrange a loan for the purchase of two more machines. I asked him if I could analyze the operation rate of all the machines at the factory before he went. It turned out that the total downtime due to sharpening amounted to 6.7% of the total operating time. In all, there were 32 turret lathes that required sharpening. So, I did the following calculation:

$$32 \times 0.067 = 2.144 \text{ machines}$$

I let the factory manager know about this figure.

"I calculated that the downtime due to sharpening is equivalent to the loss of two machines,"

"It's really that much? Wow, I guess a central sharpening system really is in order after all."

Before the week was up, an appropriate sharpening area appeared in a corner of the factory.

In this example the manager knew the problem qualitatively. Until he heard the result of my analysis, however, he did not see the problem quantitatively—time spent sharpening throughout the year was equivalent to the loss of two machines. Coincidently, this was the same number of machines he was going to purchase. Thus, using quantitative analysis in his decision making helped to prevent unnecessary spending.

Not Enough Cranes

At G Shipyard where I consulted, I suggested shortening the ship assembly time from four months to three months. At the time, the same process took England ten months and Germany seven. So, four months of assembly time was already impressive, but I insisted on shaving off another month.

Declaring the shorter assembly time was not easy. Testing its feasibility before actual construction was not an option since we were talking about a 60,000–ton tanker. Furthermore, once it was declared, falling behind schedule was out of the question as a launching ceremony with the ship owners was almost always scheduled well ahead of time.

Amidst our anxiety over planning to commit to a three month launch we were told that if the shipyard launched one additional ship by the end of the year we would break the world record for annual production. Once management heard this they insisted that we press ahead and complete the ship before the end of the year, formerly scheduled for launch the following January. Mr. N, the chief engineer of construction, stubbornly rejected this suggestion at once:

"It might be feasible in theory, but in reality it's just a pie in the sky."

I visited the shipyard and talked with Mr. N many times, hoping to convince him.

"Why don't you think we can do it?" I would ask.

"We simply don't have the crane capacity."

At that time a method called Block Construction was normally used to construct 60,000–ton tankers. About 400 prefabricated sections of the hull, each weighing about 40 tons, were transported to the building dock, lifted into place with cranes and welded together at the berth.

The engineer contended that, if the construction period were shortened, the daily number of sections to lift would surpass the capacity of cranes.

"Is that so . . . surpassing the capacity of cranes," I thought to myself. The following day I started analyzing the operation of all the cranes and discovered that the percentage of time the cranes spent lifting materials was only 25.4 percent.

I told this to Mr. N, "The cranes are moving only 25.4 percent of the time, or three months a year. In addition, 27.6 percent of the time the cranes are holding materials but not moving. That translates to 3.5 months of inactivity a year."

"Umm . . . ," the engineer uttered and turned silent.

The next day he launched a thorough investigation into the causes of the low operational rate and began implementing various measures to improve it.

Within a month he came back to me and said, "Three months is possible. Let's do it."

With this encouraging go ahead from the chief engineer, we embarked on our record breaking mission.

On the brisk morning of December 30th, 1956, the 60,000–ton super tanker, assembled in only three months, launched successfully into the water.

During the banquet, Mr. N came looking for me. He said, "I suspected that the cranes weren't operating at full capacity. But the number you gave me—only three months a year in operation—was a staggering wake up call. At that moment I said to myself, "You have to do something about this." Thankfully he did and as a result the G Shipyard broke the annual ship building world record.*

A Numerical Remedy for Ambiguous Language

Every time I visit shop floors I often think that the words we use are not clear enough. Although there are times when ambiguity is preferred over clarity, it should never be the case during work, especially on the floor.

When I visited B record factory, I asked a worker who was inspecting records, "What are you inspecting?"

"Various things," he answered.

"Could you be a little more specific?"

"Well... I'm checking to make sure that there's no dust."

Figure 17 Record Factory

"I see. And?"

"And, I'm making sure that there are no scratches."

"Anything else?"

"Nope, that about covers it."

"Various things" actually meant only two things in this case.

"Various" and "appropriate" are useful words, indeed. When asked why defects are increasing, a worker might answer, "There are various factors. We're going to take appropriate mea-

---

*As a testament to Dr. Shingo's philosophy of being dissatisfied with the status quo, by 1958 he had production time down to two months. Every shipyard in Japan soon switched to his methods.

45

sures." Will the problem behind defects actually be spotted or taken care of? No one will ever know.

"More or less" is another versatile expression that's as clear as mud. The limitation of knowledge stemming from these ambiguous terms often goes right up through the company chain of command.

If a plant worker says, "The production is more or less going well." a division head who heard this might attend a meeting and repeat it. An assistant manager at the meeting may then go and talk with clients. However, he would be completely unable to provide any details regarding the actual production. The plant manager, whom all these people report to, would have absolutely no idea what was really happening on the factory floor.

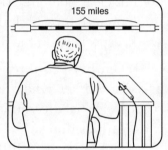

Figure 18 Annual Distance

The heart of the matter lies beyond these equivocal words and can only be found if we expend the time and effort it takes to get there. As mentioned before, presenting things with numbers is one way to help us achieve this.

At B factory which manufactures televisions, the plant manager noticed that the soldering irons were too far from some of the workers. He calculated the distance between a soldering iron and the worker who was sitting farthest from it, and multiplied the distance by the number of annual work days. It turned out that the worker was walking as much as 155 miles a year! The plant manager immediately decided to optimize the placement of the soldering irons to minimize this inefficiency. Although the plant manager may have been aware of this problem, the full magnitude of it was not apparent until he saw the numbers.

Here is another instance of numerical figures providing people the means to see problems. At G shipyard, there was a job that required workers to place five ton copper boards properly in the assembly yard with cranes. The following is the breakdown of their work:

G Shipyard Time Breakdown	Table 12
Primary placing operation	15.0%
Walking	17.0%
Attaching & detaching hooks	22.5%
Waiting for a crane	11.2%
Meetings	11.8%

After these results came in the section chief implemented changes at once, such as placing people in the assembly yard as well as in the material yard, and upgrading to more convenient hooks.

The saying "Numbers stimulate the brain," is true indeed. We should all remember this little piece of wisdom when trying to elucidate problems.

Thinking Analytically

Scientists discovered long ago that air is mainly oxygen and nitrogen, a finding that has fostered great advancements in our understanding of this familiar substance.

As stated in the opening of the first chapter, the systematic categorization of knowledge is what science is all about. This concept can be applied to quick and precise problem solving using the following instrumental steps:

- Reduce a problem into its major components

- Study each component

- Reassemble the components into a logical structure

Though they are expressed differently, these steps bring forth the same conceptual emphasis already proposed in previous sections, namely that of eliminating ambiguity and the recognition of a problem's many facets. Merely a reduction of

47

these previous ideas, the above steps represent a systematic and simplified formula for analytical thinking, a subject I will now specifically discuss in this section.

Who Needs a Freight Car Number?

The episode below occurred at K Turbine Company when, during the construction of a power plant, a construction site manager requested notice of machinery parts prior to their arrival by freight train.

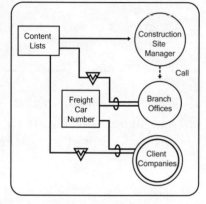

This was the pre–existing shipping method used by K Turbine's part manufacturer:

Figure 19 Bottleneck

1. Parts were divided randomly and wrapped for shipping.

2. Content lists were created.

3. The products were shipped and about two days later the manufacturer received notification of the freight car number from the train company.

4. At that point the contents list, along with the freight car number, was typed up in an official shipping confirmation letter. This process usually took 3–7 days.

5. The shipping confirmation was then sent to the parties involved.

Processes three and four caused a large bottleneck, delaying the availability of the content lists at the construction site.

To solve this problem the factory took a long hard look at the shipping process and divided it into three components: who receives the confirmation, what kind of information people actually need, and when they need it. The receiving parties are as follows:

1. Client companies
2. Relevant offices of K Turbine
3. Branch offices
4. Construction site manager

As it turned out the only person who needed the content lists before the products actually arrived was the construction site manager; proper on-site preparation was difficult unless they knew exactly what machinery parts were coming. Freight car numbers, on the other hand, was of secondary importance. Client companies and branch offices did need a record of the freight car numbers. This need, however, was irrespective of time.

After discovering this finding, the manufacturing plant changed the shipping procedures to the following:

- After contents are wrapped, multiple copies of content lists are created.

- Send a copy to the construction site manager immediately.

- After receiving notification, add freight car numbers to the content lists and send them to client companies and branch offices.

- If the construction site manager needed to know freight car numbers, he could simply call a branch office.

The key to the solution was analytical thinking. People at the factory dissected the issue of delayed confirmation into three different components: who receives the confirmation, what kind of information people actually need, and when they need it.

As a result, improvements were made that allowed the construction site manager to receive the content lists before products actually arrived, ultimately contributing to smoother operation on site.

Why Post Death Certificates?

At Y machine factory the plant manager said, "Our percentage of defects is high, around 35%. We have to do something about it."

"What kind of defects do you have?" I asked. "There are three types: material defects, design defects, and processing defects." The following is the breakdown he gave me:

Defect Analysis	Table 13
Defective material	18%
Defective design	10%
Defective processing	7%

As for the defective material, large cast iron parts manufactured at the in-house foundry accounted for as much as 18% of the defects. So, I visited the foundry. At the foundry everyone from the section chief on down was keenly aware of, and felt responsible for, the high rate of defects there. Charts of daily defect statistics were posted all over the factory office walls.

I told the section chief, "There are two ways of informing personnel about defects: you can show them 'defects,' or you can show them the 'causes of defects.'

"For example, a hole formed inside cast materials, a core wasn't centered, or the thickness was uneven—these are defects. On the other hand, poorly blended sand, moisture in the molds, and improperly placed cores—these are all causes of defects.

"Posting defect statistics is no different than displaying death certificates. Though it may instill fear and inspire caution among the workers, in all likelihood the defects will still occur since no concrete measures have been taken against them. Instead, start focusing on the cause of the problem. Every time a defect occurs, the story of how it happened should be shared with others. This way, everyone can learn what triggered the defect. Plus they can all contribute ideas for solutions. Once

50

the root cause and solution are clear, the same mistake will not be repeated."

Within three months the defect percentage at this factory plummeted from 18% to 7%. Soon after they applied this concept to design and processing as well as to aspects of production with a high incidence of defects and achieved similar results. Their newfound success serves as a poignant reminder that in order to solve problems, we must look beyond the surface; we must dig to the core — only then can we enact real change.

3 Blind Men Describe an Elephant

During a discussion on improving cost management, the plant manager of a company suggested sending someone from accounting to collaborate with someone in production.

The production manager, accounting manager, and planning manager started talking about cost management. However, the conversation quickly went nowhere because the three were actually talking from slightly different perspectives on cost:

- The production manager was talking about *cost* itself: "Those at the shop floor should take initiative in the cost cutting movement."

- The accounting manager was talking about *cost management systems*: "How do we strike a balance between managerial accounting and financial accounting?"

- The planning manager was talking about *paperwork required for cost management systems*: "We should simplify the paperwork for cost management."

Each of them had a separate interpretation for what "improving cost management" meant, which prevented clear communication on the topic. After coming to a realization through analysis, they addressed each aspect in turn and soon reached a consensus.

Managing Production Schedules

S Industries is a job shop which manufactures individually-produced mining machinery. Their manufacturing diversity was immense and included 2,000 to 4,000 different parts. Usually, parts ready for assembly would exit production at different times. Consequently, managing their production schedule was a nightmare. To combat this problem the factory embarked on a mission to improve production tracking on the shop floor.

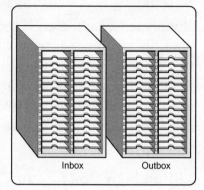

Figure 20 Job Cards

At the time their tracking system revolved around the use of "job cards." For every job assigned in the factory, a corresponding job card was created providing all the details of the work, all that is, except for one. The job cards had no place for a production time–line. Of course, management personnel immediately agreed that the addition of this information was crucial for properly tracking production. However, it had to be added in a way that was comprehensible to the workers and accessible to those managing the schedule.

A foreman suggested developing a system where each month would be divided into two boxes: "in" and "out." When a new order came in, a job card would be created and placed in the inbox for that month. Workers could then retrieve job cards as needed, complete the job and then return the card to the outbox.

The idea was certainly simple enough for the workers to understand. But with the only records of the jobs out on the floor, management would still lack the necessary information to keep a schedule.

"Why don't we make two sets of job cards, then?" one suggested.

The person in charge of creating the cards rejected this. "We make over 2,000 different kinds of parts here, but often only one or two of each. This means that at any given time, we already have 2000 or more job cards in circulation. To double that number would only cause confusion."

"How about this, then? Workers could keep only the technical drawing while on the floor and the job card itself could be put in the outbox?"

"That method would work fine," one answered, "with large-scaled parts. However, small parts, which account for about 30%, have the technical drawings inseparably printed directly on the job card. And since two sets of card are already out of the question..."

It would seem that management had found themselves in a quandary. However, this was only because they were limiting the scope of their analysis. Up until this point, their search for solutions only focused on job cards and manufactured parts. Other relevant aspects of the problem such as workers, or the machines that create the products, had not even been considered.

Someone noticed this and suggested the introduction of "machine cards" which would show information about the machines name, number, worker's name, etc. There were only 87 machines, compared to the 2000 different types of jobs. Placing one of these cards in the outbox would not only make production progress clear, the number of cards they needed to track would be reduced tremendously, making scheduling more efficient. Furthermore, workers could still retain the job cards and all the necessary information required to complete production on the floor.

The idea was just what they had been looking for. It was adopted by management and implemented as the new production monitoring system as follows:

1. Job cards are put in the inbox

2. When a worker starts manufacturing a certain part, they put a machine card, showing the completion date for the job, in the outbox's slot

3. The worker takes the corresponding job card and returns to the floor to complete the job

Without broadening the scope of their analysis, the successful conception of this new system would not have been possible. Their story serves as an important reminder that when solving problems, a truly analytical approach leaves no room for polarized thinking.

Adjusting Valves

While consulting at R rayon factory, four workers were assembling valves used for modulating the flow of a viscous solution by following this procedure:

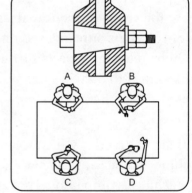

- Install an anchoring bolt through the valve housing and into the flow regulator

- Slide on a metal washer

- Fasten the first nut

- Fasten the second nut

- Tighten the nuts with a wrench

Figure 21 Rayon Factory

Two nuts are required to prevent unintentional loosening caused by the vibrations of high speed spindles operating nearby. Loss of regulator tension could potentially alter flow settings, ultimately resulting in uneven nylon. However, tightening the nuts too securely made manual adjustments difficult. Thus, only a narrow range of torque was appropriate.

Since no official protocol existed detailing the specifics of the tightening step, the four workers had to rely on their intuition to accomplish the task. Consequently, their accuracy varied greatly depending on their level of experience. The list below shows what percentage of assemblies each worker tightened correctly.

Accuracy of Assembly	Table 14
A	100%
B	80%
C	60%
D	60%

I spoke with worker A. "It seems like your adjustments are perfect every time. How do you do it?"

"I just tighten them until it feels right."

"Hmm. Until it feels right..."

Obviously this answer did not clarify anything. But as I watched her work a thought came to my mind, "Perhaps there are two separate parts she pays attention to, the tightness of the bolt against the regulator, and the tightness of the nuts against the bolt."

After some inspection of the shop floor, I noticed that the nuts and bolts were originally already assembled together. Yet for some reason in a step prior to valve assembly they were unnecessarily disassembled. I requested that they discontinue that procedure, which in turn simplified the valve assembly process. Now workers could focus less on assembly and more on proper torque adjustment.

Since one aspect of their work was standardized, it allowed worker A the freedom to instruct the others in her method.

1. Tighten the first nut to 12

2. Tighten the second nut to 10

3. Readjust both again (the first to 10, the second to 12)

Within a week the accuracy of workers B, C, D increased substantially:

Assembly Improvement	Table 15
B	100%
C & D	80%

" KNACK "

The method worker A developed through years of experience was based solely on a hunch. But in actuality, we learned that her method consisted of two key elements: 1) adjusting the tightness of the bolt to the regulator, and 2) adjusting the tightness of the nuts against the bolt. This simple observation ultimately fostered a major improvement in production efficiency. It is proof that even when applied to mundane tasks, the positive impact of analytical thinking can be profound.

Limestone Quarry Quandary

I once visited a limestone quarry of P Lime Industries. While looking out over the vastness of the quarry I asked my guide, Mr. Fujimoto, "What kinds of problems do you have here?"

"Impurities often get mixed into the raw material," he answered.

"What do you mean by impurities?"

"For instance, if clay gets mixed in with the raw material, its quality goes down. Thus, we call clay an impurity."

"So, is clay the only impurity?"

"No, there are others. Fine limestone for example, and thin layers of limestone, usually less than about 3 cm are also considered impurities," said Mr. Fujimoto.

"Limestone is an impurity too?"

"Technically it's not an impurity, but fine limestone is a problem. When burned, it clogs the kiln's ventilation system and increases the chance of producing unburned products, or defects."

"So, there are two types of impurities: clay and fine limestone," I said to myself.

While we were looking at the quarry, clay and fine limestone rejected at the factory were carted and cast away in a valley several hundred meters away. This alone seemed to be adding a significant amount of work.

We left the quarry and came to the factory where a kiln was located. Lime, which had already gone through the kiln, was spread on the floor and being sprayed with water. My guide told me that lime turns into dry power about a day after this hydration process.

"If everything is made into powder anyway, isn't there a way to make use of that fine limestone?" I asked.

Mr. Fujimoto repeated his point that it would block up the ventilation system of the kiln and cause defects.

"How about burning fine limestone in a separate kiln then? And if the current ventilation system doesn't work, could you not possibly use a ventilation machine to forcefully create air flow?" I asked.

Mr. Tokunaga, chief of the research section, joined in. "I think he's onto something, Mr. Fujimoto. We should give it a try. We'll start researching it right away. It may well lead to greater conservation of precious resources in this country." Although I do not have the result of the research at this point, if successful, the rate of wasted limestone, which was about 10%, would surely go down.

In this case analytical diagnostics of constituent elements, collectively called "impurities," helped launch a resource–saving project.

Quality Control and Statistics

A new method of quality control using inferential statistics was introduced to Japan, via the United States. Many companies benefited from its implementation by being able to infer from a sample what a total population might be. However, a state of over-dependence developed along with the illusion that quality control could not be achieved without the use of statistics.

Quality control is quite possible without any knowledge of statistics — as long as people can think analytically, the causes of problems can be deduced. After all, isn't that what real quality control is all about? Moreover, if statistics are used improperly or as a replacement for analytical thinking, it can cause havoc.

There were cases where quality control achievement was measured by the number of statistical charts created. Instead of addressing defects as they happened, people preferred to wait a month and discuss them in meetings using these charts. This not only made tracking down the causes of problems more difficult, it also created a distance between shop floor workers and management.

As I have been explaining thus far, problems will be clearer and easier to solve if we know how to observe them analytically, separate them into components, and consider each one of these components anew. Inferential statistics, or any new tool of management for that matter, is meaningless if it diverts the users' attention from the real task of quality control. When it comes to problem solving there is no tool that can ever match the deductive reasoning power of our own analytical thinking.

Giving Shape to Problems

Giving problems a concrete shape is a very powerful means to define perception. This clarifying process can be done through speaking, writing, and better yet, visualization.

The first method, speaking out, sounds simple enough. However, actually trying to describe a problem can sometimes be harder than we think. If this happens it is a sign that we still do not have a solid grasp of what the problem actually is. Nevertheless, expending the energy to think up a better description actually gives the problem a more concrete shape, and in turn, serves to improve our understanding. At the same time, just saying anything we want will not constructively lead us to this end. Therefore, to find the most direct route to a solution it is essential to avoid vague expressions.

For example, saying, "Are you feeling alright today? It looks like you have jaundice," though blunt, is far more specific and conducive to its solution than saying, " You don't look yourself today."

I was surprised when I was once told, "The entire lot was ruined today." However, the problem seemed much more manageable when more details were given: "Among the materials Mr. Koga prepared today, one lot, 50 kilograms, became defective."

Trying to give a detailed portrayal is, indeed, extremely important. In doing so we are able to clarify what aspects of problems we still do not understand.

Another way to solidify a vague problem is to write it down. Writing has certain advantages over speaking:

- Uncertain aspects of problems become even clearer

- Compared to spoken words, written words tend to be more concise and accurate, contributing to a better under standing of the true nature of the problem

Furthermore, our understanding is likely to come faster if we think in terms of the following:

- What do we know?

- What don't we know?

- What are we trying to find out?

By thinking in this way we can (a) discern problems from general situations, (b) learn what the real problem is, and (c) evaluate the problem's size or gravity against the situation as a whole. When problems appear in front of us, trying to describe them in this way first will surely put us on the fast track toward their solution.

Taking this method of clarification a step further, we arrive at visualization. Most people would agree that watching a baseball game on TV is better than listening to it on the radio. Seeing things almost always leads to a faster and more comprehensive understanding.

Take this mathematical question as an example: There are an unknown number of children. If you give 6 apples to each child, 15 apples remain. If you give 7 each, you are short 10 apples. How many children are there? Although this problem could be solved just with an equation, drawing a quick diagram as below would certainly help one's comprehension.

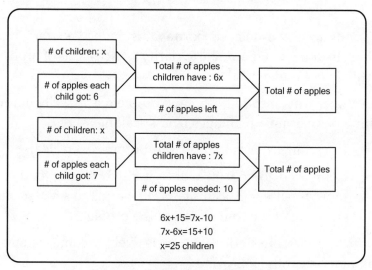

Figure 22 Giving Shape to Problems

Let's think about another problem: Workers at Mr. Akita's division decided to have a year–end party. If everyone chips in $10, there will be a deficiency of $140. If they each contribute $20, they have a surplus of $60. How much should they collect, if they want to have just enough money?

1. Given elements:

   The amount of money collected from each:

   $10 leaves the party $140 short
   $20 gives the party $60 surplus

2. The element we look for (answer): the amount of money that should be collected from each

To solve this problem, taking into account only the elements above is not actually enough. One more aspect has to come into play.

3. Hidden element: total cost

From the given elements the total number of people, x, becomes clear. However, this is not the answer. We have to divide the total cost by x to get to the final answer, y.

Number of participants = x

$$10x + 140 = 20x - 60$$

$$10x = 200$$

$$x = 20$$

$$y = (10 \times 20 + 140) \times 1/20 = \$17$$

This question shows the importance of taking into consideration factors that are not necessary given or clear at first glance.

Although only mathematical problems are used as examples here, this method of visualization can be applied to any number of circumstances. Presenting a problem with visual diagrams like the first question will leave little doubt as to its underlying framework. The illustrations at the end of each chapter in this book serve the same purpose.

As long as we ensure that every key element is incorporated, giving problems concrete shape by telling, writing, or visualizing, will greatly facilitate our journey towards comprehension and solution.

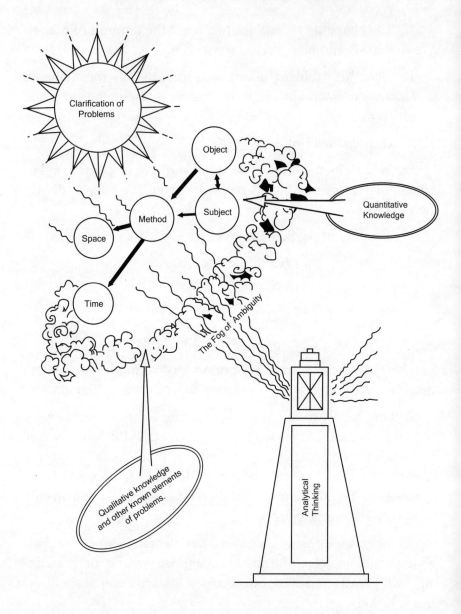

Figure 23 Analytical Thinking

To reach clarification of problems, your analysis must include quantitative and qualitative knowledge. It is the only way to pierce the fog of ambiguity.

Finding the Cause: In Pursuit of Purpose

It is said that humans are the only animals that act based on reason. In fact, every action throughout our life has purpose; at least, that is how it should be. Due to the force of habit or sheer laziness, we often act without asking ourselves "why" or consid ering the true purpose of the action.

"Why do we eat?" If this question were asked, many would answer, "To gain nutrition, so that we can enjoy a long and healthy life."

The reality may differ. Sometimes we eat just because food is there, or just to enjoy the momentary satisfaction of having food in our mouth. Even worse, we might eat a certain food because we saw it on a TV commercial, and are unwittingly serving the purpose of benefiting a company's bottom line, instead of our long term health.

For the most part, human action is based on reason. Nevertheless, we often forget our purpose or misunderstand what the ultimate purpose really is. Consciously pursuing the purpose and reasoning behind one's action is just as important in manufacturing as it is in our daily lives. Indeed, sometimes the solution to a problem is discovered only in the process of realigning our actions with their true purpose.

4 Purposes of Improvement

The purposes for factory improvement, for example, may include the following:

1. Increasing productivity
2. Improving quality
3. Cutting time
4. Cutting cost

The fulfillment of these purposes can act as a gauge for how well we are improving the factory. Conversely, failing to fulfill these purposes means there are problems that need to be fixed.

Thus, if we take the time to refine our actions on the basis of their intended purpose, problems will often disappear.

The success of this concept is contingent upon how well we identify and define our purpose. Think of the pursuit of purpose as a three dimensional concept where:

- X: represents the clear purpose of goals.

- Y: represents single or multiple purposes. If multiple, clarify each.

- Z: serves to fulfill the ideal to be reached, such as future state not–stock production.

Scratching the Surface

Knowing the job and knowing the purpose of the job are two very different things. We may know our job to the letter, but indifference or a lack of awareness as to why the job needs to be done can greatly limit our success.

True Purpose of Investigation

I was meeting with the president of N Mining Company in Kita-Kyushu when there was a knock on the door. It was Mr. Y, the mining director, and Mr. K, the accounting director. They had just returned from investigating the feasibility of acquiring a competitor's mine that was (fiscally speaking) about to go under. I offered to leave while they gave their report, but the president insisted that I stay and listen.

"Things are in terrible shape as we expected," said Mr. Y. "Their mining has been reckless and the roads and preparation facilities haven't been maintained well at all."

"Their accounting practices are just as bad," chimed in Mr. K., the accounting director. "There are many outstanding accounts; payables that haven't been paid off and receivables that haven't been collected. It's completely unorganized."

Seemingly finished with their report, the president, who had been almost silent, opened his mouth. "Is that all?"

"Well . . . yes," replied Mr. Y, reluctantly.

The president cocked an eyebrow at me, "As we all know, R Mining Company is on the verge of bankruptcy. Isn't it expected that their operations would be in dire straits?

"I didn't send you to confirm the obvious. I sent you to discover whether there's still any potential left in the mine. Of course their operations are in shambles! But it's possible there's hope buried somewhere underneath, and I expected you to dig a little to find it!"

Figure 24 R Mining Company

This episode taught me the importance of extending our thoughts beyond the job and onto the true purpose of our work, especially if it is not obvious from the given instructions. Confirming the development potential of the mine prior to acquisition was a crucial factor in the decision for N Mining to buy. Consequently, ascertaining this information was integral in the company's investigational purpose. Although not specifically instructed to do so, had the two men considered this as their purpose upon their visit, perhaps they would have returned with information that could have served the growth of their company.

Cutting Construction Time in Half

Miles and miles of traffic as far as you can see — this has become a fact of life in many places due to incessant road construction. Roads are necessities for life and I do not intend to deny the benefit of road repair here. However, every time I see an endless line of tail lights, I cannot help but wonder why it could not be completed much faster.

Construction takes longer than necessary because there are long intervals, often a few days, between each step.

Road Repair Process	Table 16
Dig up parts of the road that need to be repaired	
Take away the dirt/debris	
Make concrete by mixing sand, stone, cement and water	
Pour the concrete in and smooth out the surface	
Wait for concrete to solidify	

The entire repair could be completed much sooner if workers for all the processes are brought together at once and each process is taken care of one after the other continuously. When I suggested this approach, some raised objections. One of them said, "Road construction projects provide opportunities for the unemployed to work. If the duration of work is cut back, what are they going to do?"

I must say that this argument does not hold water. Cutting back construction time is not synonymous with cutting back employment.

Currently, road repairs are done as follows. If there is construction at five different locations, 12 workers are assigned to each site at a time, the minimum number necessary to complete one process of construction. Once the process is completed, the 12 move to the next site. Repair work halts until the workers for the next process arrive.

The following is what I suggest. Instead of using 12 workers at different locations, bring 60 to one place and complete all the processes in a single day. Once the work is finished, move the 60 to the next location. This method does not curtail employment, yet takes only one sixth of the time.

Managing personnel is easier with the current method, so construction planners are not eager to change. However, the primary purpose of repair is the convenience of those who use the road. Thus, minimizing inconvenience during the repair should be a primary concern.

I recently read in the newspaper that a machine was imported to Japan that could perform all road repair processes in a short amount of time. I believe that the duration of repair can be shortened significantly without the use of such a machine, as long as construction planners, federal or local governments in most cases, consider the real purpose of road construction and streamline the workflow accordingly.

When to Use Your Skills

While visiting a foundry, Mr. D, a veteran engineer struck up a conversation with me. "I'm not very happy with young engineers these days," he said.

"What makes you say that?" I asked, rather surprised.

"They constantly get wrapped up in technicalities. For example, they're obsessed with the milling machines. As soon as they hit the shop floor they pour all their energy into modifying the tools: changing the blade material, adjusting angles, and so forth.

"I understand the importance of good milling when finishing up products," he continued. "However, it's far more important to invest resources towards improving our casting accuracy. That way we can create products without milling in the first place; a goal this factory's had for some time.

"Even after explaining this, young engineers still obsess over milling theory. I wonder if their education is to blame."

There is a big difference between having skills and knowing when to use them. The overriding goal at this factory was to create desirable products faster and with less waste. Improving casting techniques and eliminating milling altogether would go a long way toward achieving this. Spending company resources on unnecessary improvements certainly would not.

The young engineers measured their contribution by how many skills they could use, but rendered themselves useless by squandering them on menial tasks. It is an example that demonstrates that while having skills is good knowing when to employ them is of far greater benefit.

Welding Porthole Screen Holders

During a meeting at R Shipyard, the welding process of porthole screen holders was brought up for discussion. To make a product a thin strip was cut out from sheet metal, bent to form a ring, and the joint welded together (Figure 25). This method used material more efficiently and was thus preferred over just punching the ring out of the sheet, even though welding had inefficiencies as well. The process was done as follows:

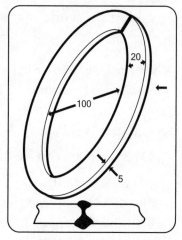

Figure 25 Porthole Screens

Porthole Welding Process	Table 17
Place ring on work table and weld one side of the joint	
Flip it over and weld the other side	
Sand both sides of welded surface	

Sanding of the back side was very important since it had to lay flush with the screen and any roughness could result in damage. However, the time required for this step was exorbitant and workers wanted to discuss ways of simplifying it; various ideas arose.

One said, "Can't we create some kind of a jig that flips them over with a foot pedal?"

Another said, "Can't we weld both sides at once?"

Amidst this discussion, Mr. Nishikawa said, "Do we really need to weld both sides? The purpose of the rings is to hold down screens, right? Screens are not heavy."

People at the table looked at each other at this idea. One said, "Sounds like a good idea. If it works, we don't have to sand the back side at all."

The feasibility test of this idea was carried out. The result was a single-sided weld that could hold screens just fine. The new method was taken up immediately.

She Fought the Lawn

A secretary came into the president's office one day and said they had a problem.

"What is it?" asked the president.

"It's about the lawn in front of our building. It seems like students from the nearby high school walk across it all the time. I posted a 'No Trespassing' sign."

"And?"

"Well, it worked for a while, but eventually they started walking across it again. After that I put up a fence, albeit a low one, as I thought a high fence would be unattractive. That was effective but not for long. They aren't children so I don't want to go out and scold them. At this point, I just don't know what to do."

"I have an idea," said the president. "It seems like the easiest thing to do would be to make a nice path through the lawn."

At times it can be very hard to find a common sense solution when, like the secretary, we focus on only one aspect of the problem. She had exhausted her options for solving the problem because it encroached upon the status quo. The president on the other hand, held a broader view and found a solution to the problem instantly.

Theory of Logical Strikes

The quality of life for blue collar workers has seen much improvement during the past few years; there is no question that labor movements, strikes especially, have played an important role in this advancement.

However, some strikes result in major personal and economic disruptions extending far beyond the nucleus of the primary participants. The effect of transit and power station strikes, for example, is tremendous. Millions of consumers can be affected. Various industries around the country can also be hit hard, lowering profit margins, impeding growth, ultimately impacting the quality of life of everyone, including the workers themselves.

Labor unions go to great lengths to explain that their actions are directed solely toward the company, and not toward the general public. Yet, many times this is not the case, which results in a loss of public support even when the principle of the strike is agreed to be valid. Is there a way for employees to have the influence of a strike without causing the public to suffer unintended casualties?

One possible answer could be deduced using the concepts of analytical thinking and considering purpose. A strike is a tool used by employees for the purpose of leveraging employers to change. Again, it is not meant to inconvenience the public. Presently, the method for striking involves the employee's discontinuation of service and the employers' discontinuation of salary payment. However, all too often this method falls short of achieving its purpose.

With the true purpose in mind, the following new method was devised. Note that it fulfills the needs of both parties involved without inflicting any damages to the general public and industries.

- Once a strike is declared, both employers and employees continue to work as usual.

- During the strike, the employer must assume that operations are down and they are losing money as a result. The actual monetary amount is calculated by a committee comprised of labor union representatives, the employers and a third party mediator. This money is then paid directly to the appropriate government (local, state, or federal).

- Employees continue to work, but wages are lost for the duration of the strike.

- The money that the company paid to the government would be infused back into the economy in ways that benefit the community at large.

This theory was conceived as a result of analyzing strikes and clarifying the purpose of strikes. This method not only creates the intended impact on both primary parties involved, but also transforms the resulting acute economic loss into a positive contribution for the general population.

Pride at the Podium

Being an eloquent speaker does not always correlate with brilliance in communication. Occasionally, I hear speakers unfold their story at the podium with great fluency, interjecting foreign words and arcane technical terms here and there. Their skill with language is most impressive, yet if you look around the audience, some are stifling yawns; others are sleeping outright and nodding their heads comfortably. Those who manage to stay awake do not seem to be following the speech.

Every time I see a similar scene, I cannot help but wonder what makes a great speech. Obviously, fluency alone is not enough. The episode below may provide insight to our answer.

Two engineers attended a course on production technology. Upon their return, they reported their findings to their boss.

Mr. N smoothly reported all the details of the course: its agenda, instructors, atmosphere, etc.

Mr. S on the other hand, though not eloquent, enthusiastically told his boss about what aspects of their production needed to be updated and how improvement could be carried out, based on what he had learned at the seminar. The information might not have been pleasant for the boss, since it included criticism of the current operation, but it had a clear and solid message stemming from Mr. S's desire to improve the factory. The boss was very impressed.

The purpose of a speech is not to make the speaker look good or smart. A speech with this intention eventually bores the listeners. Rather, the purpose is to make your thoughts clear and persuasive to others so that they can understand and empathize with you. There seem to be many people who fail to understand this simple premise. Those who pride themselves for eloquence may need to remind themselves what the purpose of their speech really is.

The Relentless "Why?"

Halving the Time of Core Preparation

At Z Ironworks, I had the opportunity to observe the process of preparing cores which would later be inserted into molds to create gas burner nozzles.

Workers were gluing core prints to the cores (see Figure 26). Core prints keep the core in place within the mold when molten metal is poured in. Once the metal solidifies, they become a seamless part of the casting. The gluing process was important; unless the prints were firmly attached they would move when the molten metal was poured, resulting in nozzles with defects.

At the factory, the gluing was done as follows:

1. Glue upper core prints to cores.

2. Bring the cores to a dry room and wait for 24 hours until the prints are firmly attached.

3. Take the cores out of the dry room and glue lower core prints.

4. Bring them back to the dry room and wait for another 24 hours until the prints are firmly attached.

This method did not seem very efficient. "Why are the cores brought to the dry room twice," I asked myself. After much deliberation, I pitched an idea to the president.

"You can probably attach lower core prints shortly after upper core prints are attached, instead of waiting 24 hours. When a core is placed inside the mold its core prints have to be attached very firmly. But when you are just attaching prints, the glue only needs to be strong enough to flip the core over to work on the other side."

The president was skeptical, but decided to conduct the following test:

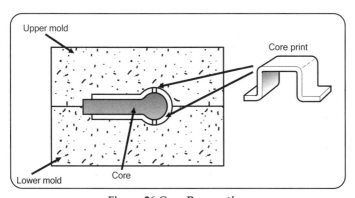

Figure 26 Core Preparation

*   Worker A attaches an upper core print to a core and sends the core down the conveyor belt to worker B.

*   Worker B then attaches a lower core print about 30 seconds later.

*   Repeat the above, then place the cores in the dry room for 24 hours.

The next day, the dried prints came out perfectly attached

to the cores and ready to be used in molds. Simply asking why and questioning the current method lead to a result that halved production time and greatly increased the efficiency of core preparation.

Increasing Efficiency of Inspections

I once observed an inspection process of water heater tanks, each about 2 meters in height and 0.6 meter in diameter. The following was the inspection procedure:

1. Use a chain hoist to lay down a water heater tank.
2. Coat the tank with a liquid detection solution to pinpoint leaks.
3. Send compressed air inside the tank.
4. Thoroughly inspect for leaks.
5. Once the inspection is done, raise the tank.

As I watched the operation, I thought about the purpose of each procedure. Applying solution reveals the location of a leak. Compressed air reveals the existence of a leak. I asked the foreman, "What's the percentage of defects?"

"It's relatively low, about three percent," he said.

"Three percent..." I mused, "Why don't you try this method then? Infuse compressed air first and check whether or not a leak even exists with the pressure gauge. If there is a leak, lay down the tank and apply the detection solution to locate it. If the defect percentage is indeed only three percent, then only three tanks out of 100 really need to lie down to have the solution applied, the rest only need the air-pressure test."

This method was implemented later and greatly expedited the inspection process.

A Chain Reaction of Whys

At a foundry I visited, I observed a process for creating molds for bearings. The wooden patterns used to make the bearing molds seemed overly difficult to remove. First, a worker tapped the pattern lightly with a hammer. If it did not loosen, he would pound harder until it came off.

"It's inefficient if I don't pound it hard," he said.

"I wonder if that's really true," I thought. While pondering this issue, I went to a machine factory where the cast bearings are actually used. Not long after my arrival, the plant manager said, "The castings we receive have too much allowance that has to be cut off."

An important question arose out of this revelation, "Is it better to loosen the wooden patterns so that they remove easier, or is it better not to loosen too much, so that the resulting castings have less allowance to be cut off?"

We should always seek answers by considering whether there are multiple purposes for the work. In this case we began with one purpose that took into account only the ease of removing the wooden patterns. Yet, there was another higher-level purpose which took into account reducing waste in subsequent procedures.

Actually, there is a purpose in every ensuing process.

Why do we loosen the wooden prints? — to make their removal easier.

Why do we remove the wooden prints? — to pour in molten metal.

Why do we pour molten metal? — to make castings.

Why do we make castings? — to creating bearings.

Why do we make bearings? — to hold engine shafts.

"Why" questions can continue in a chain like this until eventually, the ultimate purpose is attained. In this case the ultimate purpose of producing bearings was to provide "functionality for engine shafts."

To get to the core of problems we must keep asking "Why" until we reach a point where we can look at the entire picture as a whole.

Cannery Production Increase

During World War II, Japan was under much pressure to increase production output on numerous items. Cans, specifically, were in high demand. At that time they were manufactured by bending a tin plate into a cylinder, making juxtaposed folds on the ends, and hooking them together to make an interlocking seam. This seam was then soldered to make it air tight.

A cannery manufacturing chief from that period told me that the speed of production was ultimately decided by the speed of soldering.

"In the past," he said, "we could only solder about 300 cans a minute. When demand skyrocketed we were already operating around the clock, and introducing new machines was out of the question. So, we launched a major research project to improve our soldering irons."

"What were the results?" I asked.

"After much trial and error, we succeeded in building soldering irons that could make 350 cans a minute."

"That's great."

"Yes, we were very happy. However, not long after that, the war ended and I heard from an engineer in the United States that they can make 600 cans per minute there."

"600 . . . how do they do that? Did they invent an even better soldering system?" I asked incredulously.

"I couldn't believe it either. Especially since we had just imported the latest machines from the United States right before the war started. If the rate had been 400, maybe I could've believed it. But 600! That's double our number."

"But it was true?"

"Yes, it was. Though I was doubtful at first, I asked around and gradually realized that it was the truth. I tried to find out how they did it, but they wouldn't disclose their methods."

"I guess it was a secret."

"It probably was. Eventually though, I discovered what the secret was. And when I heard it I had to hang my head in shame."

"Why was that?"

"Because it was so simple; cannery machines can make various sizes of cans, from 6 cm to 15 cm in height. Back then 6 cm cans were in the greatest demand. The United States' method was to make 12 cm cans and simply cut them in half after soldering. All our effort to improving our soldering technique was not even necessary.

"Their solution was so easy and yet after 30 years in the business, I couldn't see it."

Failing to come up with this idea seemed to hit the manufacturing chief hard. He had gotten so wrapped in improving soldering that he could not see that there was a much easier way to increase production. Had he asked "why" and relentlessly questioned the current method more thoroughly, the ingenious concept might not have been so elusive.

Documents Destined for Nowhere

During a meeting at N company's branch office, issues were raised concerning the documentation of labor statistics. At the time they were required to present up-to-date information on workers' compensation, attendance, and labor hours. It was a tedious and exhaustive task using extraordinarily complicated forms.

One of the members suggested simplifying the forms to make data input and calculations easier. Another suggested consolidating it with other required documents. I started to wonder how the statistics were used, so I asked. The answer I got sparked my curiosity: "We're just supposed to send them to the regional main office."

So, while I was at the regional main office I asked some questions and discovered that documents changed hands a few times and then ended up with the human resources manager. When I talked with her however, she told me that she just sent it to company headquarters without looking.

About a week later I had a chance to visit headquarters so I decided to track down the documents there. After a while, I found out that they traveled rather aimlessly through three different departments. Still, it was reassuring to hear that they were actually used by the chief of the statistics department. When I visited the chief however, he said, "Labor statistics? Oh right, I scan the document, but I don't really use it here. I think other departments need it."

No one needed the statistics document.

I reported this finding upon my return to the on–site office and had the documents discontinued at once. I heard later that collecting the statistics had started about five years ago when an executive wanted information for a temporary research project. Once the project was over and the executive gone, the collection continued as a meaningless habit.

Fundamental improvement—elimination of the documents—was made possible as a result of pursuing the purpose of the documents through a chain of whys. If the focus had never broadened beyond scope of the documents themselves, this result would not have been achieved.

Barrage of Questions at a Brake Manufacturer
Our series of "why" questions have so far been mainly happening in vertical directions. However, we also need to be aware that these questions can likewise expand in horizontal directions.

At K industries, a worker was cutting off curved sections from brake shoes using a grinder. While I was observing, I said, "That looks like a tiring task."

"You're telling me," he said.

"Can't you use a hydraulic press instead?"

"Unfortunately no, this metal part gets in the way."

"Why's that?"

"For whatever reason these metal parts aren't flush when we get them from the supplier, and we can't make the size of this part uniform in all brake shoes."

"Why can't you make them uniform?"

"Well, actually I've been asking our supplier, T Steel, to make them uniform, but apparently it's technically difficult."

There was no point in discussing the technical problem of a different company, so I changed the subject.

Figure 27 Brake Shoes

"If the size of part B varies, why does that prevent you from punching the section out with a press?"

"Well, it doesn't work well if the press hits this metal."

"Why can't you just avoid the metal?"

"I could but I'd have to finish the metal part later and that's more work."

"Then, why can't you remove the metal part first with the grinder?"

Eventually, our "why" dialogue came to an end.

Though continuing this type of questioning can be tiring, we must try not to stop too soon, for we could end up falling short of an easy solution.

When faced with the task of improvement, inquiries based on cause and effects are extremely important. Indeed, this concept is fundamental to the method of pursuing purpose sequentially. However, when pursuing solutions using this "chain of whys," we need to be aware that our line of questioning does not necessarily have to have a cause–and–effect relationship. This type of horizontal thinking is analogous to the relation between night and day. Night comes after day, but day is not the cause of night. If we patiently expand a chain of "whys" vertically and horizontally, feasible solutions will eventually arise.

What to Light First?

I once overheard a comic dialogue while consulting in Osaka, which illustrates the ideas I am trying to convey.

"Kids these days are very smart. Sometimes, they ask questions that I can't answer. "

"I know what you mean. Isn't it embarrassing when kids know more than you?"

"I was asked a very difficult question the other day."

Figure 28 What to Light?

"Really? What was it? I bet I can answer."

"Ok, this is how the story goes. A housewife was talking with a friend and realized that she had lost track of time and evening was fast approaching. So she rushed home, but the moment she walked into the house — poof! — the power went out; it was a black out.

"So, she felt around trying to find some matches, and after some blind scrounging, she found a matchbox. But there was only one match inside and she had three things to light: a candle,

80

a gas burner, and a gas lamp. What should she light first?"

"Why, she lights the candle first, right?"

"No, no. The first thing she lights is the match."

It is a silly dialogue but nevertheless, it is analogous to what many of us do when faced with problems. Even when it seems we are pursuing our true purpose we often overlook fundamental steps that allow us to achieve it. Throughout this chapter numerous examples have shown the importance of pursuing the ultimate purpose along with methods for how to do so. However, that ultimate purpose is always made up of smaller segments, each with their own purpose in turn. It is the sum of these parts, in harmony with one another, that make it possible to fulfill that ultimate purpose. Therefore, the strategy of our pursuit cannot just end with the naming of our overall objective, it must continue, every step of the way, until our true purpose is completely realized.

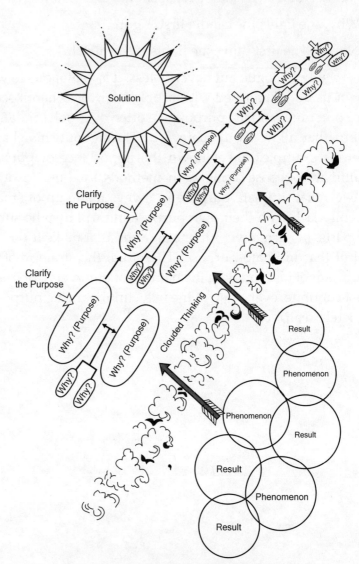

Figure 29 Chapter 2 Summary

A relentless barrage of "why's" is the best way to prepare your mind to pierce the clouded veil of thinking caused by the status quo. Use it often.

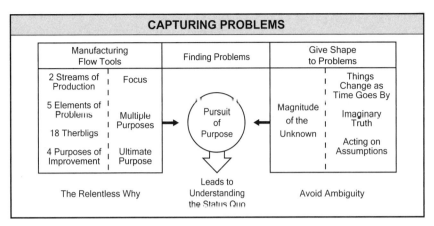

Figure 30 STM Component Chapter 2

To capture a problem we must develop it, examine it, and give it definite shape in order to understand the status quo. The Magnitude of the Unknown is an awareness tool that encompasses aspects of reality that are easy to miss, avoid, or ignore, because their very nature is embedded in the status quo. The use of Manufacturing Flow Tools gives a tangible, quantitative understanding of problems and helps to focus improvement efforts by keeping multiple, and the ultimate purpose, in mind. Asking "why" at every juncture will help to further define, refine, and focus on the problem at hand.

 **III** IDEA GENERATION FOR IMPROVEMENT

> Once the problem and the purpose are clarified, it is now time to generate improvement ideas. How do we do this?

Many Paths to a Single Summit

If we want to achieve improvement we must first have the mental flexibility to believe that even though there is only one summit, there are many paths we can tread to reach it. If we adamantly think that the current methods are the best and no other means are possible, improvement ideas will never emerge.

If employees were under the impression that the way in which they performed their job is flawed, it would be impossible to receive quality work from them. Even though the flaws have nothing to do with the employee, it is still a discouraging thought.

When asked the question, "Is there anything that needs to

be improved with your job?" five out of ten people would probably say, "No, everything's fine." The rest might say, "There might be something that could be improved," thinking that this is the expected response. But in fact, they too probably think that the current methods are just fine.

If we are reluctant to change from the beginning, it is a guarantee that improvement will never take place. There are always unexpected and better alternatives for everything, even for the little things we do without thinking. Realizing this is the catalyst that opens our minds to new possibilities, and the first momentous step towards successful improvement.

Quickest Way to Fold Furoshiki

Some Japanese people use a silky cloth called a *furoshiki* to wrap things. When they are ready to be put away, how do people fold these useful, yet unwieldy pieces of cloth? The following are the common methods.

Chin Method	Table 18
Hold corners of the cloth with hands	
Hold down the middle with the chin	
Fold in half, hold the ends with the right hand, and hold the middle with the left hand	
Lift it up and fold it in half again	

Table Method	Table 19
Spread the cloth on the table	
Hold the corners with your hands and fold in half	
Hold corners on the right hand side, and fold in half	
Lift it up	

Although the cloth can be folded in the manners described above, I would like to suggest an alternative method (Figure 31).

Figure 31 Folding *Furoshiki*

This method is much quicker than the other two and illustrates the fact that there is always another method to every task, even if it is as simple as folding a cloth.

High Speed Folding Method　　　　　　　　　　Table 20

While holding the middle of one side with the left hand, pinch the center of the cloth with the right hand and pull up

Still holding on with the left hand, reach across, and grab the other side of the cloth in the middle and pull up

---

Painless Method of Tying Boxes

At the N food factory, there was a task that everyone tried to avoid — the seemingly simple job of tying boxes.

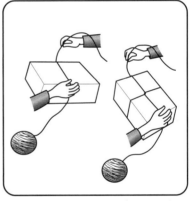

Figure 32 Conventional Box Tying

The conventional method was as follows (Figure 32).

While this method was straight–forward, the repetitive task of tightening strings was hard on the employees hands. During the dry season, some would even start to bleed.

Conventional Box Tying Method　　　　　　　　Table 21

Place a string over a box

Flip the box over, cross the string and rotate 90 degrees to wrap in a perpendicular direction

Flip over the box again, and tie the ends

Concerned about the well-being of his employees', Mr. Fujimoto hit upon an idea one night. The following is his method. This method achieved the same result yet it eliminated the need for tightening strings, flipping over boxes, or rotating them 90 degrees. Best of all this method protected the hands of the employees.

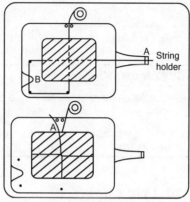

Figure 33 Automated String Tying

High Speed Box Tying Method	Table 22
Place a string as in Figure 33 Place a box on top Pull part A through part B and tie it to the end of the string	

Finding Your Marbles

I was at K power line factory to observe the paper wrapping process of wire pulled from a coil and into a machine where it was wrapped. The finished line exiting the machine was then reeled onto a drum. Though it seemed simple enough, there was a problem with this process. When the line remaining in the coil became low it did not feed smoothly into the machine. Often, loops of line would get pulled in, wrapped, and then reeled on the drum. Whenever this happened workers were left with the time consuming task of unreeling the loop, cutting it, and welding the line back together.

Until my visit, the only method devised to deal with the problem was to have a worker tap the coil when the line was low to loosen any potential tangles. Although this worked, it was exhausting for the workers since each was in charge of about 15 machines.

"Can't you create some kind of a mechanism that loosens the line?" I asked the engineer in charge of the process.

"We've been trying, but we haven't come up with anything very effective."

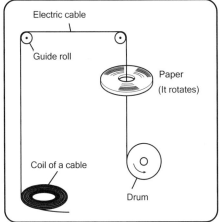

Figure 34 Paper Wrapping Process

I had the chance to observe the same process of paper wrapping cables at H factory in Kyushu. I stood and watched a machine for a while. To my surprise no loop or entanglements occurred. I wanted to see the source from where the cable was coming from, but it was enclosed in a container and I could not see it. At that moment the section chief walked by so I asked, "It looks like you don't have a problem of cables looping or entangling. What kind of secret is in this box?"

"Ah this," the section chief said, patting the top of the box, "we had that problem until about two years ago. However, our plant manager Mr. Muto, is very enthusiastic about improvement and came up with this great idea. I'll show you what's inside."

He opened the lid and what I saw inside it was an innumerable amount of marbles.

"Those are just marbles aren't they?" I asked, amused.

"Yes, just regular marbles. If an entangled line tries to get out of the box these marbles are lifted as well and they tap the line lightly. Usually that's enough to untangle the cable; isn't it interesting? It seems as if marbles aren't just for kids."

I was very impressed with this extraordinary use of marbles and the way it reminded me that there are always different ways to do our work. Even if there is only one summit there are numerous ways to reach it. In other words, there are multiple means to a single purpose.

Improvement Plans

The following are stages we need to go through to create improvement plans:

- Come up with ideas to break loose of the status quo.

- Judge and choose the best idea, and think about what needs to be done to actually implement the idea.

Development of Thinking Methods

Phenomena of Human Action	Table 23

1. **Reflex** Blinking, sneezing, coughing, yawning

2. **Instinct** Hunger, sexual appetite

3. **Conditioned Reflex** Involuntary action induced by certain conditions (Salivating when one prepares to eat something sour)

4. **Learning** Act based on knowledge gained from observation, experience, and education

5. **Deductive thinking** Act specifically based on a general theory

6. **Inductive thinking** Induce a general theory from specific actions and act based on this notion

7. **Creative thinking** Conceive something which did not exist before and act based on this idea

Human actions are induced by various phenomena. It is said that it took humans over 2,000 years to move from Aristotelian deductive logic to inductive logic, and only 400 years have passed since the emergence of inductive thought, brought about by Rene Descartes. Deductive logic moves from general statements to specific statements; inductive logic moves from the specific to the general.

While making full use of deductive and inductive logic we should all try to gain mastery of the creative thinking aspect of human action; it is ideally suited for improvements.

Mental Activities for Improvement

One scholar explains the stages of mental activity necessary for improvement as follows:

1. Focusing attention

2. Accurate observation

3. Memorization

4. Logical thinking (deductive and inductive)

5. Correct judgment

6. Association

7. Creative thinking

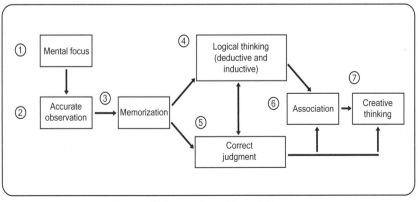

Figure 35 Seven Step Mental Process

Another scholar advocates the following, epistemological* method:

- Clarify the problem (analyze and evaluate it).

- Clarify what is behind the problem (pursue and clarify the goal of improvement).

- Do not over think (if the ultimate solution cannot be found, or further pursuit is not necessary, stop thinking accordingly).

- List all the possible solutions (compare all the options and eliminate the ones that are considered inappropriate).

- Examine what seem to be appropriate solutions and their methods of implementation (list all the means of implementation and compare).

- Make the final decision and implement (take into account the difficulty, the cost of implementation, and the expected revenue).

Scientific Thinking Approach

A well–known method for improvement is called the "Scientific Approach" or the "Experimental Scientific Thinking Approach," is explained as follows:

- Focus on the facts to be surveyed and decide the scope of investigation.

- Collect and examine all existing related records and documents.

- Observe, then thoroughly measure and record problems with the current method.

---

*Immanuel Kant is considered to be the founder of epistemological philosophy. His *Critique of Pure Reason*, published in 1781, looked at the relationship between knowledge based on reason, and knowledge based on experience. Epistemology investigates the origin, nature, methods, and limits of human knowledge.

- Analyze each measured and recorded element, identify the most fundamental problem.

- Formulate a plan to solve the problem.

- Make a schedule based on the plan.

- Implement the plan.

- Check to see if the intended outcome has been achieved.

Scientific Thinking Mechanism

Based on my 30 years of hands-on experience of plant improvement, I developed a system I call the *Scientific Thinking Mechanism.*

It embodies techniques and philosophies advocated by others such as the aforementioned Experimental Scientific Thinking, Creative Thinking, and Brainstorming methods. Although each of these methods captured a certain aspect, none of them were comprehensive. Thus, I combined the strengths of these various methods and created this systematic Scientific Thinking Mechanism.

I owe a tremendous amount of gratitude to the teachings of those who came before me for the development of this process; however, I take a certain pride in having synthesized these various concepts into a single, stronger system.

This Scientific Thinking Mechanism forms the backbone of this book and if you refer to Figure 36 as you read through it will be a valuable visual asset for comprehension.

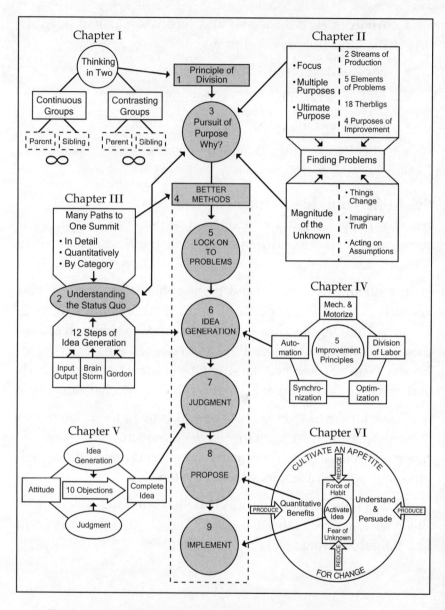

Figure 36 Scientific Thinking Mechanism with Chapter Notations

As with all scientific models, the Scientific Thinking Mechanism is a systematic representation of an idea and how that idea works. In this case the idea is idea generation from inception to implementation.

Scientific Thinking Mechanism
Table 24

1. **Principle of Division and Problem Awareness** It is necessary to have a solid understanding of the principle of division. It is also important to have an awareness of problems.

2. **Understanding the Status Quo** Make sure we understand the status quo, and avoid accepting assumptions based on guesswork or on things that may have changed over time as facts. Even if we think we understand the current situation, we have to do so in detail, quantitatively, and by category.

3. **Pursuit of Purpose** Make sure we ask the questions "Why" and "What for" thoroughly, and pursue the purpose from three dimensions: X, Y and Z.

4. **Finding Better Methods** Keep an open mind and seek new methods. The motto is "multiple means to a single end."

5. **Locking in on Problems** It is important to have the freedom of mind to entertain doubts about the current methods. Question everything.

6. **Idea Generation** Use the "Steps of Idea Generation" to generate ideas freely. Think in groups at this stage and take full advantage of its merit.

7. **Judgment** Keep idea generation separate from judgment; make a judgment after all the ideas are on the table. When evaluating complete ideas, remember to differentiate the purpose and the means. It is important to accept objections as a warning and to understand the "10 Ways of Evaluating Objections."

8. **Proposal** After judgment, propose the improvement plan while taking into account its effect and cost.

9. **Implementation** In order to translate the improvement plan into reality, gaining understanding of others is not enough; they have to be persuaded. Effort needs to be made to overcome the force of habit.

Of all the stages above, locking in on problems and idea generation play the most important roles in bringing forth successful improvement.

Be it a factory floor or an office, I believe that this Scientific Thinking Mechanism can be applied anywhere. Moreover, it has tangible advantages over all other methods in the fact that it can be measured by real changes in production output resulting from faster and more effective improvement.

Methods of Idea Generation

Considerable research has been done examining different methods of idea generation. Many concepts presented in my method exist as a direct result of this research, some of which are summarized below.

Brainstorming

Brainstorming was developed by A.F. Osborn in the United States. It is based on the following ideas:

- Humans can produce more ideas in group settings rather than thinking individually.

- The power of idea generation is greatest in a criticism-free environment.

According to an experiment, when the same topic is presented, 44 percent more ideas were generated in groups rather than by individuals alone. This can be attributed to the chain reaction of thoughts created in group settings. One person's idea stimulates another's through the process of association. According to psychological experiments of adults, a range of 65 to 93 percent more associations occur in group settings.

For effective brainstorming it is important to maintain an environment where creative output is encouraged. During the brainstorming meetings the following four rules must be observed.

Four Basic Rules of Brainstorming	Table 25
1. No criticism 2. Welcome unusual ideas 3. Generate as many ideas as possible 4. Combine and improve ideas	

The first rule, no criticism, speaks for itself. It is by far the most important rule as it is the foundation through which all others are applied.

The second rule, welcome unusual ideas, comes from the fact that unusual ideas promote new ways of thinking and more often than not, lead to better solutions.

For example, there was a brainstorming session at a company on the topic of improving toasters. One participant suggested the idea of attaching mouse traps to their toasters! This bizarre idea eventually lead people to realize that accumulating bread crumbs were to blame for attracting mice; therefore, a mechanism to take out bread crumbs should be installed. The company responded by inventing toasters with removable bread crumb trays and their sales rose sharply as a result.

The third rule, generate as many ideas as possible, comes from the simple fact that if there are more ideas, there are more great ideas.

The fourth rule, combine and improve ideas, is an essential component of group-intelligence stemming from the comprehensive association and synthesis of ideas.

In addition to following the previous rules, the following should be considered prior to brainstorming:

Problem

- Define the problem, it needs to be clear and not too big.

- The target should be challenging. Dynamic results can be expected if the topic is "cutting the rate of defects in half" rather than "reducing defects by 10 percent."

- The problem should be something that does not require pen and paper. Problems that require writing down equations or calculations are not appropriate.

- The problem needs to be presented in a clear and distinctly simple manner so everyone can grasp the issue at hand.

- The problem must not be disclosed beforehand. If back ground information is needed, reference material can be used.

Participants

1. Five to ten people are ideal.

2. It is better to mix people with various backgrounds. It is also a good idea to combine those who are outspoken with those who are reserved.

3. Groups can be all males, all females, or mixed gender.

Time

1. 30 minutes to an hour is preferred but it can be as short as 10 or 15 minutes.

2. If the session is planned to last an hour, insert a short break (about five minutes) in the middle and take a rest from thinking. Any break longer than 10 minutes is not appropriate, as it will diminish the established momentum.

Session Process

- The facilitator explains the four basic rules.
- The facilitator explains the problem clearly and suggests a few leads.
- Have a camera or recorder on hand to document the session. It is also a good idea to have a whiteboard available to present the ideas visually.
- If the flow of ideas stop, the facilitator should suggest more ideas or hints to rekindle the session. If criticism is raised and continues, the facilitator should give a warn-

ing and reiterate the first rule.

- If the participants seem to be tired, the facilitator has to make an effort to change the mood by throwing in appropriate jokes or relevant stories.

- The table for the meeting should not be too big. Small tables create a better atmosphere for discussion.

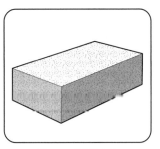

Figure 37 Brick

- A relaxed atmosphere should be created. If all the participants can pitch in their ideas in an enjoyable manner, as if they are playing sports, the session will be a success.

Brainstorming: **Common Brick**		Table 26
Weight	Color sample	Stand
Anchor	Wheel stopper	Kettle trivet
Tea pot trivet	Flower pot stand	Teaching
Marker	Target	material
Gatepost name	Carving material	Carve into
plaque	Break apart for	an ashtray
File	gravel	Pencil sharpener
Whetstone	Grind into sand	Use to color cement
Chalk substitute	Use as weapon	Use to demonstrate
Heat and use as	Sample at a brick	a rectangular shape
foot warmer	store	Insulation
Display for a	Use for shot–putting	Pillow
brick maker	Shore up unstable	Ruler
Step	table	Hammer
Block a mouse hole	Use for making a	Book end
Cut into pieces for	brick wall	Cutting board
building blocks	Grind into powder	
	to use for blinding	

Brainstorming: Sheet of Newspaper

Table 27

Wrapping paper	Raincoat	Use as seat
Place under area rug	Body wrap for warmth	Ice wrap
Origami paper	Toilet paper	Toilet seat shield
Hat	Sunscreen	Curtain
Book cover	Table cover	Protect food from flies
Moisten it to clean with	Mix with modeling clay	Make Paper-Mache
Packing material	Dry shoes with	Tissue
Fuel	Burn to collect ash	Recycle
Cut out sewing pattern	Use it to show paper sizes	Use as a gauge
Calligraphy practice paper	Cut out words for blackmail letter	Font size sample
Font type study material	Kanji character study material	Kana orthography study material
Use as table shield while gluing	Masking paper for painting	Advertisement study material
Advertisement sample	Writing study material	Layout study material
Pickpockets use it to cover hands	Pick up something dirty with	Fly swatter
Material for paper culling craft	Research material for ink types	Clean up knives and razor blades
Wrap a box lunch	Trivet	Kindling
Use as a bellows to get a fire going	Use as a chimney	Teachers use to find cheaters (cut a small hole in it and pretend to read)
Use as right angle sample	Use as standard of weight	Use it to make a duster
Make confetti	Paper tape	Use to absorb cooking oil
Blotting paper	Bookmark	Shoji screen material
Lamp shade	Dustpan	Fan

Brainstorming is not necessarily a thinking method meant for improvement. Rather, it is a style of thinking and idea generation that can be used for improvement but it is also applicable for broader purposes.

There is a well-known Japanese saying that states, "Out of the counsel of three comes wisdom." This old adage echoes brainstorming in terms of the effectiveness of collective thinking.

I sometimes use brainstorming to encourage creativity. I once asked people to come up with more than 100 ideas on the topic of "things that can be achieved with 30 seconds of manual labor." They immediately thought it was impossible. I explained the rules of brainstorming and asked people to discuss in groups of three. At the end of the session, as many as 680 ideas were presented.

Some of the participants said, "Now I understand just how much judgment acts as an obstacle to creativity in our daily life."

It is vital to keep judgments from the brainstorming process. Indeed, it is the essence of brainstorming. For this reason, I emphasize the importance of collective thinking and the separation of idea generation and judgment in my Scientific Thinking Mechanism.

Input–Output Method

The Input–Output Method is a technique used at General Electric. It works by first clarifying the issue at hand and then thinking about the following:

- Input
- Output
- Conditions

Take sun shades for example.

- Input: Energy of the sun, light and heat
- Output: Filtered portion of light and heat
- Conditions:
  - Finished products have to fit windows of all sizes
  - Filtered light cannot be more than 20 candle power

- Cost is less than $40 per window

Once these three variables are defined think about their relationship to input and output and how the input might be adjusted or controlled to produce desirable output. For example:

1. What kind of phenomena do heat and light cause?

    a) Heat changes water into vapor

    b) Heat expands gas and metal; it melts some solid materials

    c) Certain materials move or bend due to light and heat

2. How can the above effects be used for sun shades?

    a) Steam produced by heat

    b) Bimetal bending

Thoughts could be developed in this manner to create new ideas. In this case, one possible outcome uses the bending characteristic of bimetal to turn on and off electricity and adjust the shade electrically. This method explains the Scientific Thinking Mechanism of: 1) understanding the status quo, and 2) the pursuit of purpose stages, using the concept of input, output, and condition.

Gordon Method

The Gordon Method is similar to brainstorming, except for the following aspects:

1. Only the facilitator knows the problem, not the participants

2. The subject given is related to the real problem but broader, the real problem should not be explicit from the given topic

For example, if metropolitan parking limitations is the real problem, the topic given to the participants might be 'storage' as opposed to 'parking.' Conditions would also be given which, in this case, might be as follows:

- The smaller the storage space, the better
- What is inside has to be able to come out easily

Participants may discuss different styles of storage which exist in nature, at home, and in factories: "How about beehive-style storage?", "How about hanging, as you would to hang clothes?"

Once the discussion has advanced considerably the facilitator reveals the true issue. Then, the panel revisits the ideas and deliberates if they could be applied.

The downside to this method is that it is difficult to conduct and success depends greatly on the skill of the facilitator. Moreover, this method is considerably more time consuming than brainstorming, often requiring up to three hours or more.

However, if these shortcomings can be overcome this method can have great potential for creating completely new and unique ideas.

This method corresponds with the "Pursuit of Purpose" stage of the Scientific Thinking Mechanism.

Other Methods

There are other methods as well such as the "Focal Method" or the "Catalog Method." Also, when the number of participants is large, brainstorming can be done in two stages: The first stage is a brainstorming session in groups of six, and the second stage is a discussion of the ideas brought together by the brainstorming.

Whatever the method the basic rule of separating idea generation from judgment must be observed.

Association is the Mother of Ideas

Oftentimes when we hit upon new ideas we assume that it is an original inspiration when in all actuality this is not entirely true. New ideas are often just different combinations or modifications of what we either have experienced before or have learned from others. We may not realize this simply because memories are often tucked away and hidden within our subconscious mind.

New ideas are simply products of association based on pre-existing knowledge. In psychology, these associations are divided into the following four types depending on the contexts in which ideas might be associated:

1. Similarity: An association of ideas caused by similarity in size, purpose, or time—dogs and cats, bikes and motorcycles, plums and cherries. In other words, remembering a past experience similar to the current stimuli or circumstance.

2. Contrast: Remembering a past experience contrary to the current stimuli or circumstance—night and day, East and West, good and evil, up and down.

3. Contiguity: Remembering a past experience contiguous in the current time or space—desk and chair, summer and swimming, school and teacher.

4. Cause and effect: Remembering things that have a cause and effect relationship—typhoon and flooding, cigarette butts and fire, economic depression and unemployment.

Our inspiration is merely a reincarnation of past experiences that is summoned by associations taking place in our mind. In this sense, it is extremely important to have a group with wide and varied experiences. Every experience adds to the source of ideas.

12 Steps of Idea Generation

Up until this point I have explained various methods of improvement — understanding the status quo, pursuing the purpose, and varying our thinking style. These methods by themselves however, are not idea generation techniques.

In this section, ways of formulating ideas will be explained in detail. The basis of idea generation is still association, therefore, if we know how to induce associations constructively, we can easily create innovative ideas for improvement. The following are the 12 Steps of Idea Generation.

1) Eliminate — Can the Process Be Discontinued?

Eliminating processes while achieving the same ultimate goal — this type of improvement plan is not always appropriate. However, if it is possible, you can expect very effective improvements. Again, it is important bear in mind the ultimate purpose.

Welding Rod Management

Welding is the main construction method used for ship building. Consequently, an enormous amount of welding rods are constantly required on hand. As a result, the management of these rods is a constant source of headache at any shipyard.

At the G shipyard, when Mr. Akiyama became the new section chief in charge of rod management, the company decided to hold a meeting to implement a new management system.

The main problem with managing welding rods was that about 35 percent of rods sent out to the floor came back. There were two types of returns:

1. Rods that are only partially used

2. Rods that are not used

As for the used rods, it was decided that thorough research on the effective use of rods should be conducted. The second type of returns, unused rods, was a more complicated matter.

1. They had to be returned to appropriate places according to their type and size.

2. Before they were sent to the floor, rods had to be dried in a machine. Naturally, returned rods would have to be re-dried in order to be brought out to the shop floor again, resulting in a redundancy of work.

Above all, when unused rods were returned it was often not documented properly. This created excess stock since the inventory quantity could never be specified.

At the meeting it was proposed that unused rods should be reported properly using a certain form. Various opinions were exchanged on its specifications:

"The form would be used on the shop floor, so it should be as simple as possible."

"It should list all rod types and sizes so that it will be easier to tally them later."

"If the format is too big, it may become too cumbersome."

Amidst this heated discussion Mr. Akiyama, who had only been listening so far, said "It sounds like you are focusing on how to handle returns. Can't we talk about how to prevent re-turns? If all the rods sent out are used in the first place, that will solve everything."

At this insightful comment everyone turned silent for a moment. The discussion was focused on the implicit premise that returns were unavoidable. They were actually avoidable however, as long as the following could be accomplished:

- Make a clear and detailed plan for the following day

- Establish a standard for rod consumption for each process

Making a clear plan beforehand had been difficult in the past, but now the company was at the point where management of the hull assembly process was advanced enough that the work of the following day could be spelled out in detail. Participants of the meeting agreed and started to discuss the issue from a new angle.

The discussion took a new course from there.

Even if returned materials were to be managed well there would be no end to the management work itself. Eliminating returns altogether was a far more fundamental way to solve the problem.

Wire Core

At the K foundry, wire cores were brought up as a topic of discussion. At the time workers who needed wire had to bring material from storage and fashion it themselves using a hand-operated twisting machine at the corner of the plant.

This inefficiency became so obvious that a group of section chiefs started tossing around different ideas.

"Why don't we assign one person the job and make all the wires at once?"

"Why don't we upgrade the hand-operated machine to a powered machine?"

Mr. Hiromoto, who happened to be there, said, "Excuse me, isn't there a way to have the wires made at a wire factory?"

"Right, that's an option, isn't it?" The section chiefs agreed and promptly asked the procurement manager to call a wire factory for feasibility.

The wire factory representative said, "Sure, we can do it. It's a very simple production for us." The company cordially agreed to take on the job at a cost that turned out to be 5,000 yen cheaper per month.

This favorable result would not have been achieved were it not for the simple suggestion of eliminating the process from the in-house factory altogether.

Coil Assembly Adjustment

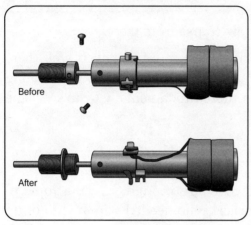

Figure 38 Amplitude Coil Assembly

At the R radio factory, there was a tedious process for attaching threaded rods into amplitude adjustment coils.

As shown in Figure 38, the task involved placing a metal washer and two screws on the upper and lower side of the coil body to fasten down the threading rod inside the coil. The work required handling tiny parts and was very exhausting.

Concerned about this inefficiency and the demanding nature of the work, a foreman set out to reinvent the task. After much deliberation about the purpose of the process he realized that metal washers and screws were not actually necessary; the threaded rod itself could be screwed directly into the body of the coil.

This innovation not only eliminated the need for handling tiny parts, it also increased the speed and simplicity of the process.

Flange Stock Control

H Pipe Factory had a recurring shortage of pipe flanges necessary for production. The plant manager Mr. Harada, said, "In the past we often ran short of flanges and the pipes waiting for parts would pile up in a heap on the floor.

"We recently started a new system; when job cards are issued, workers go to the storage room and have the store manager make sure that there are enough matching flanges in stock.

"That was somewhat effective and the amount of pipes waiting for flanges decreased significantly. However, if there were manufacturing delays the workers would end up retrieving the flanges a few days after checking the inventory. As such, matching flanges would still run out of stock because they'd get used on different pipes."

Clearly, having the flange inventory under control was a real challenge. Furthermore, the store room where the workers went back and forth for parts was on a different floor, adding unnecessary motion.

Based on the opinions of those involved, the factory decided to formulate an improvement plan. At first, the following points were clarified:

1. Even when flanges are out of stock at the pipe factory, the company's main factory usually has them in stock.

2. When a shipping request is sent out to the main factory, it takes two days for parts to be delivered.

3. The daily output of pipes usually does not show much fluctuation.

Based on the information above, the following improvement plan was put in place:

- Have the main factory send one weeks' worth of flanges, based on the past record of consumption.

- When the remaining inventory is down to three days, the store manager contacts the main factory to request the next shipment.

- Formulate a daily standard of flange consumption at the shop floor. If extra parts are required, notify the store manager three days in advance. The manager then contacts the main factory to request shipping.

- The store manager makes a chart of daily flange consumption. If there is a major fluctuation, adjust the maximum and minimum inventory level accordingly.

Once this new system was implemented not only did the problem of stock out disappear, but also the overall inventory at the factory became significantly leaner. The success was achieved due to the drastic change of thinking. The factory went from making workers confirm availability of stock to having a proper system in place so that the stock is always available.

A Doctor's Office

I went to visit Dr. Koizumi for the treatment of a migraine. Looking at my health insurance card he said, "Efficiency Consultant. Exactly what kind of work do you do?" This question broke the ice and our conversation quickly settled on the topic of plant improvement.

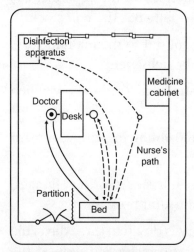

Figure 39 Doctor's Office Before

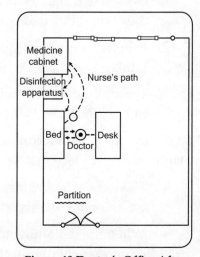

Figure 40 Doctor's Office After

The doctor was intrigued. "Interesting, I didn't know that such a job existed. Do you think you could do something for my office? It's become very difficult for me to move about in here." Dr. Koizumi had injured his leg in a car accident and it was now painful for him to walk. The office was arranged as in Figure 39. I thought about ways to minimize his walking and suggested the new arrangement shown in Figure 40. The new arrangement liberated the doctor from walking back and forth between the bed and his desk. In addition, the distance the nurse had to walk was reduced by about two thirds.

2) Perspective — An Opposing Viewpoint

Inspecting current methods from an entirely opposite perspective is another effective method of idea formulation. Take Amanohashidate for instance, one of Japan's three most scenic places. It is said that the true beauty of this place could only be experienced by literally inverting one's perspective and viewing it upside down, between your legs.

Weighing Castings

After casting, finished products are always weighed and compared against the original material weight, to see how much was lost from shrinkage or from waste metal removal. At a railway factory there was a process of weighing cylinder liners, each of which weighed more than 50 kilograms. Two workers would place a pipe inside a cylinder and yank it up onto a scale. After recording the weight, they would have to hoist it back off the scale.

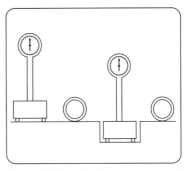

Figure 41 Pipe Scale Improvement

Mr. Eto, an assistant manager, realized that there was room for improvement with this procedure and suggested a new method: bury the scale so that the measuring surface was flush with the floor.

By changing the way he looked at the process, Mr. Eto was able to come up with an idea that simplified the task significantly making it possible for a single worker to roll a cylinder on and off the scale comfortably.

111

Tweedle Dee & Co.

At a building berth of G Shipyard, I was having a conversation with Mr. Ono, a veteran engineer who had been serving the shipyard for more than 40 years.

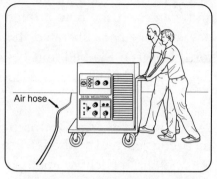

Figure 42 Mobile Welding Machine

During the conversation two workers came toward us pushing a mobile welding machine on wheels. There happened to be an air hose lying in front of them. When they saw this obstacle they decided to lift the machine over top of it. While they were struggling with its weight, two more workers walked by and offered to help.

At this Mr. Ono turned around. He quickly walked up to them saying, "Just a second…" and hoisted the air hose over the machine with ease.

The problem was gone and we left the workers standing there bewildered.

The Metric System and Price

When the metric system was introduced to Japan, volume and weight based pricing experienced extensive changes. For example, what was "100 monme = 250 yen" became "200g = 133 yen." Looking at this type of change, I could not help but wonder why they made the weight exact instead of the price.

If prices are not exact, the exchange of money becomes needlessly complicated. Adjusting the weight of goods is far simpler, "225g = 150 yen" for example, and is easy to adopt for products sold in bulk like beef and sugar.

We go through unnecessary troubles like this everyday. Solutions might very well be staring us in the face, waiting for us to reverse our perspective so we can utilize them.

Radio Assembly

Attaching intermediate frequency transformers is an integral part of radio assembly. At the Minatomachi plant of R Industries, the process was done as follows:

- Insert the legs of a transformer to the base
- Flip over the base and screw it down from the bottom
- Insert the second transformer to the base
- Flip over again and screw it down

Note that with this protocol, the base had to be flipped over twice. Unhappy with this repetition of tasks, the plant manager Mr.Nakamura, succeeded in inventing a jig (see Figure 43) that would allow two transformers to be set in place upside down. As a result, the task was reduced to just two steps: (1) place the transformers in the jig, (2) screw down the base which is placed upside down and on top of the transformers.

Figure 43 Transformer Assembly

Aside from the transformers, many other radio parts were also installed through the underside of the base. By changing his perspective to consider a completely upside–down assembly, Mr. Nakamura designed something that not only improved transformer installation, but also comprehensively improved the speed and ease of the entire assembly.

Battle of Antietam, September 1862

During the American Civil War President Abraham Lincoln ordered General George McClellan to take the Army of the Potomac to meet the Confederate Army of Northern Virginia, under the leadership of General Robert E. Lee, before they could enter Washington D.C.

Lincoln had 87,000 troops, yet McClellan was reluctant to face the 55,000 strong Confederates. McClellan's argument being that "two troops in defense are worth three troops in offense."

Lincoln was contemplating how he could break this stalemate when an anecdote from his childhood sprang to mind.

One day as a young child, he was having trouble putting on his long socks. Even though he was pulling hard, his feet would not go in smoothly and the socks kept snagging on his toes.

Seeing him struggle, his mother came to help him. She rolled his socks inside out, put his foot in one of them, and then rolled it up.

"What I need to do is to reverse the socks," Lincoln thought. He went back to his subordinate and said, "General, you said two in the defense is worth three in the offense. That means you can defend against the enemy with two-thirds of your troops. Therefore, I will give you 29,000 troops to be used for defensive measures here. The other 58,000, I will take with me and go on the offensive to disrupt the enemy."

The timid General McClellan blanched at this idea and reluctantly set off to meet General Lee. In this way, Lincoln used the method of reverse thinking to solve his problem and break his stalemate with McClellan.*

3) Deviation – Managing By Exception
Managing through exceptions can prove itself effective in various situations.

---

*Editor's note: The Union was victorious in the battle, but not without severe losses due to McClellan's cautious nature. Lincoln fired him and actually took control of the Army for three months until a suitable successor was found.

Attendance and Absence

At Y Industries, I was asked to improve the flow of payroll clerical processes. The first step involved observing the staff members' morning duties, which were done in the following order:

- Organize workers' attendance tracking cards in order of employee number.

- Stamp "Attendance" on each card.

- Take out the cards of those who were previously absent and stamp the cards in accordance with the types of leave: absence, paid leave, or public holiday.

The last procedure seemed somewhat out of place, so I asked why it was necessary. The answer I received was, "Everyone takes their attendance cards home, so the cards of those who are absent are not here on the day they are gone. We can't make the entries on the cards until they return to work."

This seemed very inefficient so I suggested leaving the cards in a box at the factory's entryway. However, opposition was raised at once.

It seemed that N City, where the factory was located, might as well have been called Y Industries City. The company was the backbone of the entire local economy, so much so that their employees enjoyed various perks such as 20 percent off movies and other discounts at a wide range of businesses. Some would even allow installment payments for purchased items. All of these things were available simply by virtue of being an employee at Y Industries. However, to receive the discounts the workers needed to present proof of employment, i.e. their attendance cards.

Obviously, this made the attendance cards very useful outside the factory. So, I thought about how the cards could be kept at work while preserving those benefits. After some deliberation I realized that the attendance cards were simply being used as IDs. Other than that, the cards had no other functions outside of the factory.

Based on this finding I changed the system so that the previous month's cards could be retained for use as IDs and the current month's cards could be kept at work. This change provided the following benefits:

- The cards of those who were absent could be updated that day, instead of waiting until they returned.

- Additional tasks resulting from workers forgetting their cards was eliminated.

Two new In and Out boxes were placed at the entryway. When the workers arrived in the morning, all they had to do was insert their card in the appropriate slot corresponding to their number. This act alone greatly liberated the payroll staff by eliminating the tedious work of organizing the cards in order of employee number.

Already we had achieved a significant improvement. However, the issue of stamping "attendance," "absent," or "holiday" on the cards, was still problematic. After all, there were 6,000 employees, so this alone took six workers about an hour each day to complete.

While I was thinking about the purpose of stamps, this simple fact dawned on me: "absent" is equal to "not in attendance." Similarly, "attendance" is equal to "not absent."

I made the following proposal to the section chief, Mr. Ohno: "How about just stamping 'absent', and discontinue stamping 'attendance'? Then, attendance would be implicit by the lack of a stamp. The rate of attendance is about 97 percent now, which means the staff members would need to stamp only 3 percent of the cards, about 180. That should expedite the work significantly."

"That's an interesting idea. Let's give it a shot," Mr. Ohno adopted the idea at once.

There was slight resistance to change at first. Some complained that cards without any stamps seemed to lack authority.

However, once the new system was in place, the outcome was better than expected. It reduced clerical processes by as much as 40 percent.

Managing via the exception—in this case, managing attendance by absence—proved very effective. Moreover, I believe this method can be applicable in many other situations.

Time Clock

This is a dialogue I had during my lecture at B Company.

"I noticed that a time clock is used at your company. Those who come at 7:40, 7:50, or 8 o'clock sharp, all punch in at the time clock. Can anyone tell me why?"

"It's to keep track of attendance," one said.

"I see. Do you get incentives for coming early, maybe 5¢ per minute? For example, if you punch in at 7:40, do you get $1, or if its 7:50, do you get 50¢?"

"No, it doesn't work like that."

"That's too bad. At D industries, those who arrive by eight simply move their card from "Out" to "In" and don't need to punch in at all. Since the gate is closed at eight, only those who are late have to enter through security and punch their cards in the time clock."

"In other words, if people come in before 8:00, their exact arrival time is irrelevant. Time only becomes an issue if they are late. After they introduced this system, long lineups at the punch-in station just before the start of the workday disappeared."

"With success like that without punching in, and without the need for incentives, why continue to do so here?"

Three Types of Boxes

When carrying small parts, it is much easier to put them in a box rather than carrying them by hand. These "transportation boxes" are very convenient vehicles for handling all kinds of tiny and delicate items in the workplace.

A very useful type of transportation box is one that contains a fixed amount of items, appropriately called a "fixed-quantity box." For example, there could be boxes that contain 200 rivets, or boxes that contain job specific quantities like 200 cotter pins and 200 washers.

If fixed-quantity boxes are used, counting in the middle of processing becomes much easier. For example, if there is a material or processing defect in a lot of 200, the number of non-defects can quickly be specified by counting only the defects.

One step beyond fixed–quantity boxes, we have another type of box, called an "operations box." These boxes are transportation boxes specifically designed to be used as a part of a work station.

By using these characteristics of boxes well, work efficiency can be improved significantly.

Indexed Inventory

There are many office supplies designed to streamline clerical work. Among the ones that have been around for some time are indexed organizers as shown in Figure 44.

These types of organizers are great for inventories. All part names are visible and in terms of ease of use, it is much better than the conventional notebook-style inventory. With the conventional inventory, users have to go through page after page to find the section that lists the parts they are looking for.

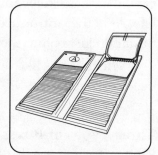

People who have been in charge of inventory and are very familiar with the notebooks may have no problem finding the information desired. However, if they happen to be absent and a new

Figure 44 Indexed Inventory

person has to fill in, there will likely be great difficulty looking up anything: "Which book is it? Under which section is this part listed?" The simplest of tasks could take a long time.

Needless to say, being able to display headings of part names is definitely a plus. But there is another, often overlooked, advantage with these neat organizers that is actually more important. It is the ability of the indexes to present not only the names, but also the ease with which they can show information most essential for inventory control, such as stock status (including ordered items, items running low, and out–of–stock items) and dates of part delivery.

For proper stock control, paying close attention to the following is essential:

- What needs to be ordered
- What items are running short (If so, a reminder for shipment has to be sent out)
- What items are already out of stock

It is also convenient if we can tell when and how the actions related to the above need to be taken.

Only items that require immediate attention or actions like above should easily become apparent. In other words, if the indexed inventories are used well, they will open up the possibility of managing stock by exception. This approach has far more value than presenting part names all at once, yet not many seem to take full advantage of its functionality.

4) Adaptation — Two Categories of Phenomena

In this world, all phenomena can be divided into two categories: things that change and things that remain unchanged. A phenomenon with a variable nature is naturally more complex than one with an invariable nature.

Solutions can arise by asking ourselves the following questions:

Can we somehow change variable to invariable?

Is there an aspect of invariability in things that we think are variable?

Weighing Powdered Milk

A factory in Hokkaido had a process in which workers would weigh powdered milk and sugar using metal containers of various sizes, and blend them together. While I was watching the process I noticed that there was a chart near the scale. I asked Mr. Watanabe, the section chief, how the chart was used.

"Ah, the chart. Well, the weight of each separate container is different. We used to weigh them individually prior to every measurement but realized how inefficient it was. So our foreman, Mr. Nishiyama, measured the weight of each container, numbered them, and made a weight chart."

"That's a great idea."

"Yes, the work is much simpler now that we don't have to weigh a container every time."

"That's good," I agreed. As I stood there watching the work however, I could not help but wonder why the chart was necessary at all. It only seems useful because the containers weigh differently.

I made a suggestion to Mr. Watanabe. "What do you think about this? Since we know the weight of each container, why don't we attach weights to lighter containers so that their weight will match the heaviest one?"

"Hmm, that's a great idea. I say we put it into action immediately."

This improvement eliminated the need for checking the chart every time and made the process even faster and easier than before.

Biscuit Cans

When I went to tour the T biscuit factory, I saw stacks and stacks of cans, each about the size of a five gallon bucket. They were lined up along the wall in one corner of the factory to a height of at least ten feet. Each can had a number written on it with a permanent marker, such as 358 or 339.

I asked my guide, Mr. Iwamoto, what the cans were for.

"We store biscuits in 5 kg units. These cans are used for measuring and then for storage. Since the weight of each can is different, we weighed each one and recorded the value on the side."

It was certainly better than weighing a can every time, but even so, having to constantly reference a different weight still seemed inefficient.

Then I made this suggestion: "Why don't you measure out 5 kg of biscuits using a single can and then transfer them to a different can for storage?"

This idea was soon adopted and put into effect. The factory also upgraded the scale to a hopper scale so that biscuits would slide down easily. These improvements greatly increased the efficiency of the whole process.

Flat Bar Bending Operation

The process of bending flat bars for oil tanker frameworking had employed conventional vertical-style presses. However, changing dies according to the type of a curve was quite cumbersome.

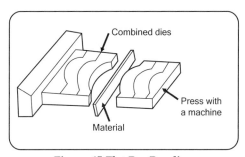

Figure 45 Flat Bar Bending

C shipyard had implemented an ingenious improvement for this process:

121

- Use a horizontal-style press to make replacing dies easier.

- As shown in Figure 45, use "combined dies", so that any die can be ready for use any time.

This method made replacement of dies extremely easy and more than doubled their efficiency.

Fixed Deduction

Companies with long histories tend to have many items deducted from salary statements. It probably comes from the fact that they have many welfare facilities and the company paternalistically deducts some items for convenience, even though that may not be officially required.

While the B shipyard was on a mission to streamline their clerical work, an issue regarding this complicated deduction system was brought to the table.

A thorough inspection revealed that there were as many as 35 different deductibles. Since there were 8,000 employees, this calculation alone added up to a significant amount of work.

In the hope of somehow reducing this inefficiency, deductibles were divided into two categories:

- Deductibles of a fixed amount per employee each month

- Fluctuating deductibles

As a result, it became clear that only 18 out of the 35 were actually fixed.

So, they consolidated these 18 items into one and named it "fixed deductions." Twice a year, in April and October, employees received a detailed breakdown of this deduction.

The monthly calculation of these 18 items was cut back to just one. Since there were 8,000 employees, it naturally made clerical processes much simpler.

5) Proportion – Keeping Size in Mind

Items that are very large, like a 1,000 kg steel plate, or an items that are very small, such as tiny screw or the tip of a pen, can add difficulty to the work simply because of their extreme size.

Tiny Pen Tips

In fountain pen production, creating quality tips is the most important aspect. If tips are not perfectly symmetrical, the pens will never write well. At one company, skilled workers were assigned to this process to create the best products possible.

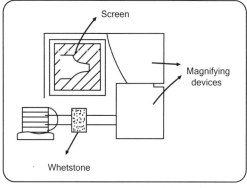

Figure 46 Fountain Pen Magnifier

However, the smallness of the tips was a challenge even for the most skilled of workers.

Naturally, finished tips were inspected using a magnifier. During production however, it was distracting to use magnifying lenses over and over. As such, workers tended to rely on their naked eyes, a practice that led to more frequent defects.

Some time after this problem was identified the company succeeded in inventing new equipment (Figure 46). The equipment would illuminate a pen tip and then, using a lens and a prism, display a magnified image of the tip on a screen alongside an image of a standard pen tip. Needless to say, this improvement increased the processing speed and boosted the quality of their products magnificently.

Cardboard Boxes and Air

It is said that storing cans for products such as powdered milk

123

and biscuits is similar to storing air – the containers are overly bulky for the contents. Cardboard boxes have similar characteristics. Yet, they are a little better since the material is paper.

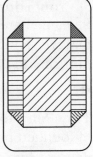

At the R factory I visited, I was impressed that the boxes ready for use were stored flat (Figure 47). When I visited the F factory, however, their method of handling boxes impressed me even further.

Figure 47 Flat Box Storage

The method was as follows (Figure 48):

1) Make boxes on the mezzanine level of the first floor directly above the area the product is being boxed.

2) Send finished boxes down a chute directly to workers in charge of boxing.

This arrangement had various advantages:

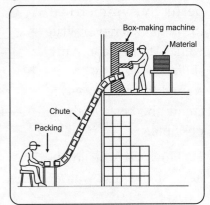

Figure 48 Just In Time Box Manufacturing

a) Boxes were stored flat, so they did not take up space.

b) Only about one dozen boxes were prepped and on standby in the area above the chute.

c) Only boxes intended for storage would have products inside.

With these many advantages, this clever approach contributed to the efficient use of their storage space.

This is an example of how "scaling down large items" can be used as a method for idea generation.

Boxing Blankets

At Q Electric Company boxes used for their electric blankets were previously made in a subcontracted factory and then delivered. Even though this method worked well enough, transporting empty boxes was highly inefficient, since 90 percent of the load was air.

To turn this situation around the company redesigned their system as follows:

Boxing Blankets	Table 28
At the end of the electric-blanket production line, place a box-making machine brought from the subcontractor	
Have a worker from the subcontracted factory come over, make boxes on site, and send them down a conveyor	
Box finished blankets immediately after they come out of the production line	

This improvement greatly benefited both factories: the subcontractor's transportation became much more efficient and it eliminated Q Electric's need to store empty boxes.

A Medicine Factory and its Location

In the production of pharmaceutical products it is often the case that the containers are heavier or bigger than the products themselves.

K Pharmaceutical Company takes advantage of this notion well. They manufacture liquid concentrates of vitamin supplements in Osaka, and then transport it in tank trucks to Tokyo—where the market is. In Tokyo, the concentrate is formulated into a supplement drink, put into glasses, boxed, and sold.

6) Distribution—Consolidate or Disperse

We can expect interesting results if we look at each phenomenon from the perspective of consolidating or dispersing aspects of processes.

Paid Holiday Application

A company initially used two forms for conventional paid-holiday applications (Figure 49). Upon close inspection, you will notice that the only differences on these sheets are the parts enclosed in boxes. This is obviously a waste of paper. So, the company which used the above format introduced a consolidated application sheet as shown in Figure 50. In this format both redundant sections and essential information are consolidated well.

Paid Leave Notices

Paid Leave Notice
Feb. 29. 2007
Dear Mr.Kato,

I am writing to request four days of paid leave from March 1st to 4th, due to medical reasons. Thank you for your consideration.

Engineering Dept.
Division of Planning

Shigeru Takemoto

Paid Leave Notice
Jan. 7. 2007
Dear Mr.Kato,

I am writing to request a paid leave on January 8th, due to personal reasons. Thank you for your consideration.

Engineering Dept.
Division of Planning

Shigeru Takemoto

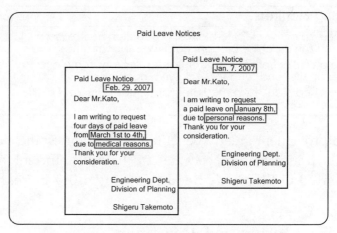

Figure 49 Paid Leave Notices

Multiple-Entry Notice

2007 Paid Leave Notice Employee #: 117

Date of Employment	Paid-Holidays			Job Title	Name
June, 23,1958	Carry Over 4	This year 20	24	Secretary	Shigeru Takemoto

Date of Request	Date	Paid Leave: Duration	Paid Leave: Remainder	Absence	Reason	Self	Foreman	Subsection Chief	Section Chief		
1/7	1 - 8	1	23		Personal resons	Takemoto	○	○	○	○	○
2/28	3 - 1 3 - 4	4	19		Sick	Takemoto	○	○	○	○	○

Figure 50 Multiple-Entry Notice

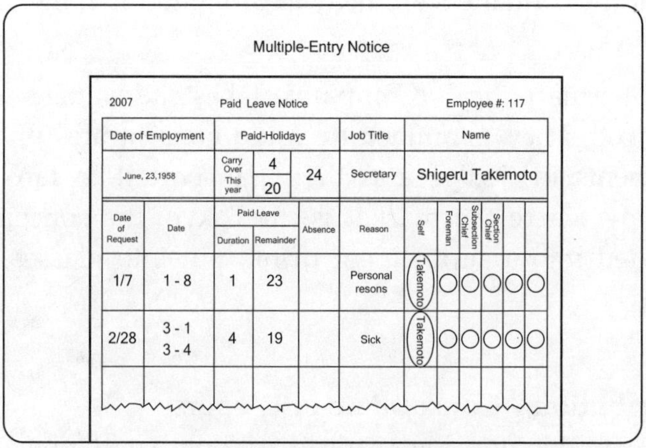

The new format has the following benefits:

- The amount of paper consumed is reduced by 95%.

- The employees remaining paid holidays are clear, so trouble stemming from confusing this information can be avoided.

- Those who manage the forms can easily track each employee's history of paid leave.

This same format can also be applied to notices of absence. Management can understand what type of leave each employee is taking, allowing for the provision of better support suitable for each individual.

Removing Laminate Distortion

Laminates for electric motors were made using a machine press that would punch the parts out of silicon steel plates. Often, burrs and distortion resulted as an unfortunate side effect from the cutting process. Naturally, these flaws would have to be removed.

During my visit to the shop floor of K Electronics Company, I walked by an operation where workers were doing just that; using a roller machine to smooth out the punched laminates.

I noticed that as the workers busily stacked the parts, they were selectively flipping some of them over. Apparently there was a top and bottom side to each piece and when parts came out of the machine their orientation ended up being completely random. If pieces came out face up, they were stacked as they were. If they came out face down however, they had to be flipped over before stacking.

After some observation, I suggested trying the following method:

- If parts come out face up, stack them as they are.

- If they come out face down, also stack them as they are, but separately from face–up piles.

127

- After the machine stops, flip over the face-down piles at once.

Once the workers switched to this approach, their job, which they had been doing in haste, became much easier.

7) Functionality — Boosting Efficiency

Many jobs involve tasks with repetitive movement, such as picking up a screw and tightening it; or hooking, connecting, and cutting wires. If a comprehensive tool can be conceived for such continuous tasks, a boost in work efficiency is guaranteed.

Pliers, Screwdriver, and Snips

In shoe production there was a process for attaching adhesive coated elastic coverings to the exposed surfaces of insoles. At one shoe factory, the work was done in the following order:

- Beginning at one end of the insole, attach the covering while pulling it taut with pliers.

- Pound the attached portion with a hammer to ensure secure adhesion.

Due to the elasticity of the coverings, proper adhesion could only be achieved by minimizing the lag time between attaching and pounding. Thus, throughout every inch of progress, workers were constantly alternating tools to properly pull and pound the covering into place.

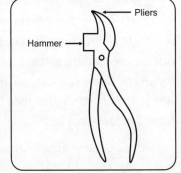

Figure 51 Plier-Hammer Tool

A member of the company, Mr. Ikegami, devised a solution for this problematic repetition by combining the functionality of pliers and a hammer together into one simple yet effective tool (Figure 51). This invention not only freed workers from the exhaustive movements used when exchanging tools, but also boosted productivity to more than double.

One laborious aspect of assembling small parts, such as components for sewing machines or clocks, is the attachment of tiny screws. Trying to do so by hand is extremely difficult; yet using tools like tweezers takes too long.

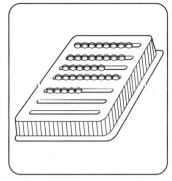

Figure 52 Screw Organizer

At one company the following method was adopted and resulted in a noticeable increase in efficiency:

- Place screws into an organizing tray with narrow slits that allow the threads to fall through and suspend the screw's head up (Figure 52).

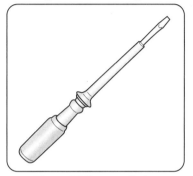

Figure 53 Forceps Driver

- Gently tilt the tray to remove any excess screws. Grab the screw with the extendable, spring–loaded forceps of a special driver (Figure 53), and place it at its attachment point on the designated part.

- Once the screw has started threading release the forceps, and tighten as necessary.

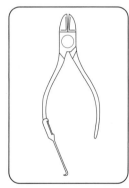

Figure 54 Snip & Hook Tool

This driver exquisitely combines the functionalities of both actions required for this type of assembly.

In radio and TV assembly workers are repeatedly pushing aside cables, attaching new ones, and cutting the excess off with snips. Conventionally, this work was done using two tools: a hook and a pair of snips. At R electronic factory however, they designed a pair of combination snips which led to a striking increase in productivity (see Figure 54).

Sectioned Container

Ideas for improvement can also arise from the inverse concept of separation. Managing small items in large quantities always poses a challenge. One clever way to achieve this is to use the concept of separation. This is illustrated in the following example by a container sectioned into two bins labeled A and B.

- Place a bag of parts in each bin.
- Take parts from bin A as necessary and record their removal on the inventory tag.
- Inventory can be cross-checked when the remainder of A becomes low.
- Once A runs out, start using from B side.

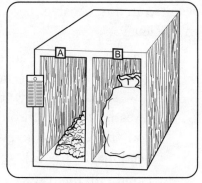

Figure 55 Separation System

This simple separation system is a powerful tool of part management. Inventory is easy to track and old parts are not at risk of permanently sitting at the bottom (which is often the case when not using separation).

Using separation also works well for storing things like steel plates. By stacking vertically in two different sections, and using up each section alternately, the problem of bottom plates rusting, inherent with horizontal stacking, can be avoided.

8) Economy — Making the Most of Motion

When analyzing the economy of motion and processes, effective solutions can arise from either adding a certain element to a process or eliminating a certain aspect of a process.

Recharging Batteries

The battery recharging process at a railway plant involved transferring batteries back and forth between a cart and a charging stand (Figure 56). Previously, the method of transfer was as follows:

- Lift battery from the cart and place it on the floor.

- Transfer battery from stand to cart.

- Lift the battery on the floor and place it on the empty slot of the stand.

Note the lifting to and from the floor that this method required. Since each

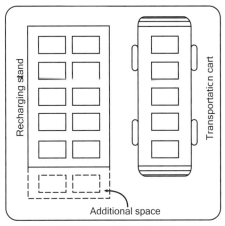

Figure 56 Battery Transfer System

battery weighed roughly twenty pounds, this was particularly laborious, not to mention risky, due to the potential for spilling the hazardous chemicals inside. However, these concerns were eventually overcome by the change in procedure that resulted from simply adding extra space to the charging stand. The following was the new transfer procedure:

- Move a battery from the cart to the additional space on the charging stand.

- Move a battery from the stand to the empty space of the cart.

- Replace the removed battery with one kept in the additional space.

This little addition eradicated the need for batteries to be

131

placed on the floor and greatly reduced the risks of spilling and back injuries.

New Screws

When trying to tighten a screw, resistance can sometimes cause the driver to slip out if the notch on the head is too shallow. Exasperated by this annoying problem, Henry F. Phillips modified a screw with an additional perpendicular notch that, along with the corresponding driver, provided much better grip over conventional flat-head screws and drivers. This of course, is how the Phillips head screw came into existence.

Bulleted Lists

Sentence flow is critical in any area of writing, be it fiction or non-fiction. Good transitional phrases are often essential, especially when adjacent sentences convey very different ideas.

However, I believe that it is more important to spend time and energy on presenting ideas clearly, rather than conjuring up nice transitions. A useful way to achieve this is through numbered or bulleted lists.

Itemizing ideas in this manner has the following advantages and works very well in office documents.

- The main point is unmistakable
- The number of points is obvious
- Key points can be easily differentiated
- The overall structure is simple

I should add however, that there is a certain downside to lists in that it makes for rather dry reading. Therefore, you may want to avoid applying this technique to your love letters.

- Spring time has come
- Its warmth has penetrated my heart
- You are my sunshine, Ms. A

Itemizing ideas as a list is a great writing tool, as long as we know when to use it.

9) Direction — Finding Flow

Electrical circuits have connections in parallel and in series, each with their own appropriate use. Reviewing working arrangements from a similar viewpoint may also prove useful in idea generation.

Rotary Drill Jig

The conventional method of making bushings is as follows:

- Hold a metal cylinder with a vise

- Bore a hole with a drill

- Detach the finished bushing

Using a rotary drill jig can make this drilling much more efficient. With the jig, the drilling process would be as follows:

1. Fill the jig with metal cylinders and drill A while it occupies the upper right hand corner. Then rotate the jig 90 degrees and drill B.

2. When B is finished, rotate the jig 90 degrees and while C is being drilled, remove the finished bushings in A and B.

3. When C is finished, rotate the jig and fill A and B with fresh cylinders while D is being drilled.

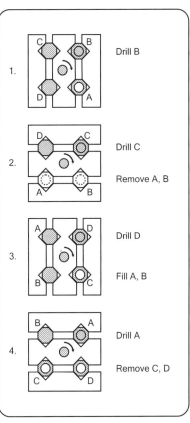

Figure 57 Rotary Drill Jig

4. Once D is finished, turn the jig 90 degrees, drill a hole in A, and remove the finished bushings in C and D.

5. Repeat the above cycle.

This method allows multiple processes—boring, setting, and removing—to take place in parallel. It can greatly improve the operational rate of drilling machines and can easily double productivity. This rotary-jig method will prove itself particularly effective when used on machines that require relatively long set-up times, such as lathes, milling machines, and planers.

A rotary assembly table, like the one shown in Figure 58, is another tool that enables efficient parallel processing. There are eight assembly steps which are required to complete each coil. Workers used to individually do all these tasks in a series, completing one coil at a time. This device, however, allows workers to focus on one aspect of assembly at a time. This is similar to division of labor and it is a far more productive assembly method.

Figure 58 Rotary Assembly Table

Pouring Soap

In soap manufacturing, the solidification process involved pouring soap into large molds, or trays. One factory poured soap into molds two square meters in size that were spread out on the floor. Once the soap inside solidified to a certain degree they could safely be transferred to shelves for the remainder of the curing process. This conventional method had some drawbacks:

• It required too much floor space

• It required carrying heavy loads

To remedy this, the following method was devised (Figure 59):

- Start with the molds already on the shelves.

- Hoist up the melted soap with a machine and pour it into the upper-most mold.

- When the mold is 90 percent full, the soap spills out through a spout and into the next mold below.

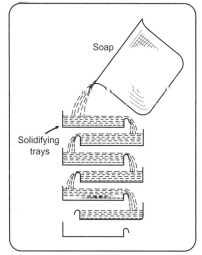

Figure 59 Soap Trays

- This cascade continues through seven tiers of molds until all are filled.

This method required neither excessive space nor heavy lifting. Not surprisingly, after its implementation work efficiency improved dramatically. In this case, remarkable improvement was achieved by modifying the operational style from parallel to series.

Arrangement of Tanks

Just as they had always done, K Milk Company arranged its milk storage tanks level with one another. However, when they constructed a new factory they decided to introduce a tiered arrangement and interconnect them with pipe.

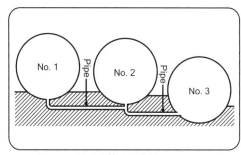

Figure 60 Milk Tank Arrangement

This layout made the management of milk much easier. Now, when milk came in, workers only needed to be concerned with the highest tank, No. 1. Conversely, when milk shipped out, only the status of the lowest tank, No. 3 was important.

10) Rearrange — Switching the Order of Operation

Ideas for improvement might unexpectedly be formulated simply by rearranging our order of operation.

Kerosene Heater Screens

R Spring Manufacturing Company produced screens for kerosene stoves (Figure 61). Their production was done in the following conventional order (Figure 62):

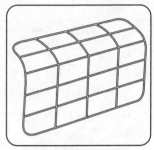

- Bend the outer frame (a), and vertical wires (b).

- Using a jig, create a lattice by overlapping the horizontal and vertical wires (b and c) within the frame (a) and spot weld the connections.

Figure 61 Heater Screen Assembly

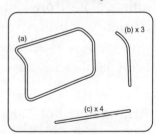

- Remove the screen from the jig and smooth out any distortion.

However, simply by rearranging the operational order to the following steps the company realized marked improvement over the conventional method (Figure 63).

Figure 62 Heater Screen Parts

- Without bending, place the wires and frame (b, c, and a) in the jig and spot–weld the lattice connections.

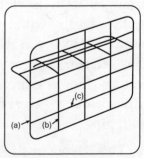

- Bend the upper section of the assembled screen with a machine press.

Figure 63 Conventional Assembly

136

- The process of fixing distortion was eliminated.

In the improved method of step one bending and step two assembly and welding, are reversed. With this simple switch in sequence preparation time was reduced and production increased.

Minty Fresh!

After washing my face one morning, I added a few drops of concentrated mouthwash into my glass of water to gargle. I looked around for something to stir it with, but nothing was handy.

I stood there thinking, "Should I use the handle of my tooth brush, or maybe just my finger?" After some thinking, I placed a hand on top of the glass and shook it. It was not the best idea I ever had. The next morning I had a better idea: put a few drops of mouthwash into my glass first and *then* pour water. The problem of mixing vanished, simply by switching the order.

Bearings of Threshing Machines

Grain threshing ball bearings were assembled using the following established method:

- Place the balls into grease

- Take out the greased balls and place them, one by one, inside a bearing until all 18 are housed taking care not to let them spill out

- Insert a shaft

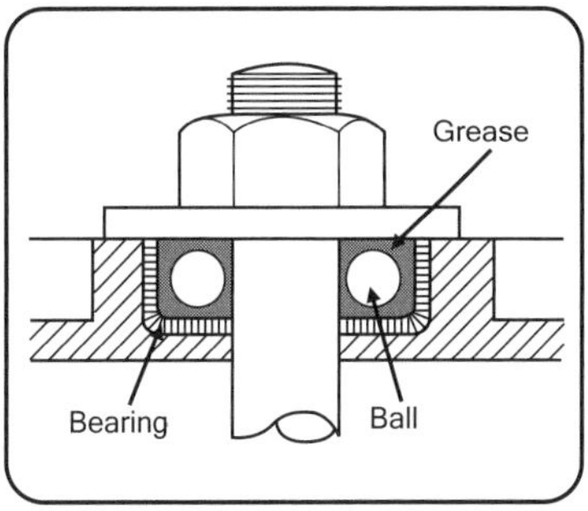

Figure 64 Threshing Machine Bearings

This operation saw great improvement after switching the order to the following:

- Insert a shaft through a bearing

- Place all 18 balls inside the bearing, around the shaft

- Pour in grease, and put on a lid. Grease will evenly distribute with a small turn of the shaft

Thus, the same result was achieved only easier and faster.

Date of Manufacture on Boxes

Boxes of food always have a manufacturing date stamped on them to show when the food was made.

At the R factory, workers initially stamped the dates on boxes while they were still flat. From there they would assemble the box and then fill with product.

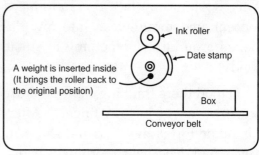

Figure 65 Date Stamping Process

The factory switched the order and improved the operation as follows.

1. Shape cardboard into boxes without stamping dates

2. Pack the products

3. As the boxes move down a conveyor belt, dates are stamped automatically with a machine

The new method provided the following advantages which simplified the work:

1. The discrepancy between the number of boxes with dates and the number of boxes actually used disappeared

2. Separate work for stamping became unnecessary

Efficient Burglary

I have heard that rearranging operational order can even be useful for improving burglary techniques. A story goes that novice burglars tend to open chests of drawers from top to bottom. Experienced burglars, on the other hand, reverse the

138

order and open from bottom to top.

The reason is if drawers are opened from the top, each drawer has to be shut before opening the next one. If they go from the bottom there is no need to shut the previous drawers, therefore it saves time.

Burglary and efficiency — it is indeed an absurd yet interesting connection. Let me conclude that there are no boundaries in the application of these idea generation methods.

11) Comparisons — Similarities and Differences

We often encounter the need to differentiate front from back, or automatically separate something long from something short. Using the concept of comparing the similarities and differences of objects and processes is a very effective way to handle these challenges.

Metal Shavings

A factory that produced machine parts had an operation for facing off the bottom of nuts so that they would sit well.

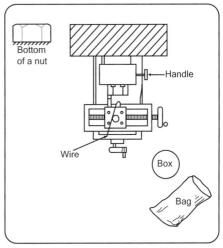

Workers would bring 10-kilogram bags of nuts from storage and smooth the bottom sides using a nut facing machine as shown in Figure 66. The following was the order of work:

Figure 66 Conventional Metal Shaving

1. Attach a nut to the machine

2. Grind the bottom part of the nut

139

3. Release the nut from the machine by pulling the handle of the machine

4. Pick up the nut with a wire as it comes off and transfer it to a box

5. Once the box is filled, transfer the contents into a bag

After observing the operation for a while, it became clear to me that this procedure was not the most efficient. For one, the wire sometimes failed to pick up the finished nuts and secondly, accumulating the nuts in a box and then transferring them to a bag seemed redundant.

So, I came up with a better alternative (Figure 67): a chute that transfers released nuts from the machine directly to a bag. With a little effort I constructed a prototype and tried it out on the machine. To my delight it worked very well.

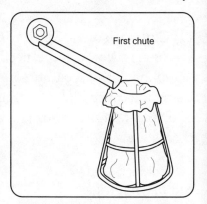

Figure 67 Shavings, First Chute

Content with the improvement I went back to my office. However, no later than ten minutes after my return, my phone rang.

"There is a slight problem with the chute you made. Could you come back down to the factory? " said the person on the other end.

I headed back the way I came, all the while wondering what it could be.

Back on the shop floor, I was told that not only the nuts, but also the shavings of the nuts, slid down the chute into the bag. "Shavings in the bag; that is a problem," I said and mulled over my next option.

The desired outcome was to transfer only nuts, not shavings, to the bag. With this in mind, I asked myself, "What are the differences between nuts and shavings?" The first thing that came to my mind was size: nuts are bigger than shavings.

Figure 68 Chute Made with Netting

If I make a chute out of netting, shavings should fall right through, I thought. I made a new chute with netting material and put it in place of the first chute. As I expected, it worked well.

Relieved, I went back to my office. About 30 minutes later, however, I got another call from the factory—"We still have a problem. Little shavings do fall through the netting, but larger twisted shavings don't and end up in the bag."

"Well, what else can I do now?" I mused to myself. Then I realized that there was one more difference between nuts and shavings: weight. "If the weight is different, the impact they would make when they hit something must also be different," I thought.

Figure 69 Eccentric Disk

As a way to selectively block shavings with lighter impact, I placed an eccentric disc between the chute and the bag (Figure 69). The following was the outcome:

- When shavings hit the disc, it did not move and blocked them from entering the bag

- When nuts hit the disc, it gave way with the force of impact and let them fall into the bag

The chute finally yielded the expected result. In this case, by taking into account the differences of size and weight, gradually lead me to the right concept.

Sorting Door Hinges

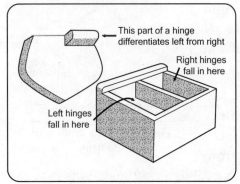

Figure 70 Sorting Door Hinges

K Industries had a process for sorting door hinges based on right side use or left side use. Since the parts were as–cast and almost identical, there were frequent mistakes in sorting.

To remedy this, a manufacturing engineer devised a simple, yet effective sorting tool as shown in Figure 70. With this tool, workers were able to separate left–sided or right–sided hinges simply by placing them on top of it. This sorting method was easy and mistake–proof.

Cutting Steel Rods

At a casting shop, there was an operation of cutting long steel rods into multiple pieces for casting. Each rod, five meters long and about 70 millimeters in diameter, was cut into 270 millimeter long sections.

To keep track of how many rod sections were made, a counting meter was linked to the cutting machine's arm and recorded its vertical movements.

However, there was a slight problem with this counting method. There was always a short piece at the end of each five-meter rod, and unless the next rod was inserted right after the end, the machine cut through thin air, yet the meter still counted it as a cut.

When this happened, the operator had to manually fix the counter; constantly having to pay close attention to the counter, the machine, and the remainder of the rod was exhausting.

The company recognized the need to change the method of operation and asked me to lend my expertise. The goal was to let the meter count only when the machine cut material, not when it cut through the air. I asked myself, "What part of the machine is associated with the actual cutting, but nothing else?" Then, I had the idea of linking the counting meter to the stopper of the machine. The stopper halts the incoming steel rod in place to make sure each cut is uniform. By attaching the meter to the stopper as opposed to the blade, shorter pieces never reached the meter.

The method was tested and turned out to be a great success. This improvement freed the operators from the concerns of manually adjusting the counting meter.

Is that So?

On my visit to a gear factory, I saw gears being scattered around the shop floor. I suggested organizing them better and keeping the floor tidier.

The chief replied to my suggestion by saying, "We've tried a number of improvement suggestions before, such as stacking or boxing the gears. The fact is, there are just too many sizes of gears and none of those suggestions improved anything."

At this I countered, "Then, why don't you use the holes in the gears to hang them on bars?" This idea used the commonality of the gears instead of their differences to create a solution that quickly solved the problem of the disorderly shop floor.

12) Redefine — Reclaiming Wait Time

Whether it is for meetings or for trains, waiting is an inevitable and often inconvenient aspect of life. Though we can never eliminate it completely it is important to formulate ideas to minimize waiting, and to think about ways to redefine this time and reclaim it for good use. In doing so, what once was an inconvenience can turn into an opportunity for productivity.

There are several types of waiting on shop floors:

1. Wait times stemming from having to wait for another worker

2. Wait times stemming from poor inter worker co-ordination

Regardless of which type of waiting occurs, it will always be associated with either of the following subsequent types:

- Waiting with full hands

- Waiting empty handed

Attaching Paper Seals

At a tobacco factory, paper seals were affixed on the top of cigarette packets. As shown in Figure 71 (A), workers used to hold a tray of adhesive seals with the left hand, take one seal at a time with the right hand, and attach it to a cigarette packet.

The efficiency of the operation easily doubled when the seal tray moved in front of the cigarettes, as shown in Figure 71 (B), so that both hands could be used simultaneously to seal the packets.

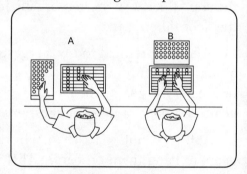

Figure 71 Seal Tray

Using Our Feet

Efficiency often improves greatly by incorporating our feet into the operation. In particular, using one's foot when a lot of hand work is required during assembly can improve the ease of operations significantly.

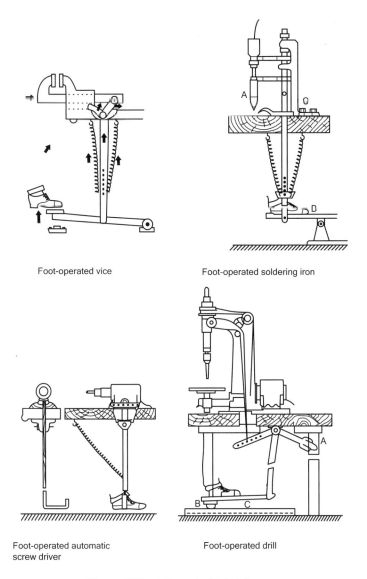

Foot-operated vice

Foot-operated soldering iron

Foot-operated automatic screw driver

Foot-operated drill

Figure 72 Foot Operated Machines

Punching Out Panels

On my visit to S agricultural machinery, I observed an operation of punching out side-panels with a press. The job sequence was as follows:

- Bring a sheet from a stack of work pieces on the left and

place it in the press

- Punch out the panel

- Place the panel in the product storage area on the right

Separating the two stacks of materials created unnecessary wait time in production by leaving the worker empty handed until they could turn around and repeat the operation. To minimize the wait, materials were consolidated to one side of the press, as shown in Figure 73. Now workers could simply feed finished panels, via a guide into a storage bin. Moreover, no sooner did they let go of a finished panel than a new work piece was inserted into the press. Because of the minimization in empty handed wait time, productivity increased by 70 percent.

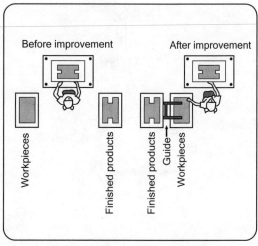

Figure 73 Workcell Improvement

X Marks the Spot

When people are asked to produce new ideas for improvement, ideas may dry up very quickly. This does not mean that those people lack ideas. Oftentimes, what is lacking is a proper education on idea generation strategies. Trying to discover new ideas in the absence of strategic direction are as futile as a shot in the dark. However, knowing idea generation strategies and applying the techniques behind them can evoke the production of powerful new ideas easily.

Thus far, I have presented 12 strategies of idea generation. It should be noted that there are many more just as useful strategies that are worth knowing. These strategies are like keys to a locked chest; the more keys you have, the greater your chances are of opening up a treasure chest of ideas.

Ideal Conditions for Idea Generation
In general, ideas cannot just be conjured up anywhere, at any time. In the following section I have outlined some ideal conditions that are conducive to idea generation.

Focus Our Minds
If we want to generate new ideas the first thing we need to do is to concentrate on what we want to accomplish. For example, if we narrow our focus by saying, "I'm going to improve this welding method," instead of vaguely hoping for change, the chance of actually generating new ideas is much higher.

According to a brain surgeon there is an area within our mind, unrelated to physical movement or the senses, called the "silent area." It is within this part of our brain that ideas are born. Just below this there is an area called the thalamus which is responsible for basic human emotions. If the thalamus is stimulated the silent area will follow and along with it the formulation of new ideas. The act of focusing our mind serves as a catalyst for this stimulus and greatly increases the likelihood for inspiration.

Providing more concrete goals such as setting deadlines or assigning distinct individual tasks, also increases the stimulus to the brain to generate numerous, as well as better, ideas.

Timing is Everything
It is said that the best time of the day for idea generation is morning, since our brain is refreshed after a good night's sleep. For this reason, setting aside the first hour of the workday for thinking is wise.

Going through documents is a very judgmental process.

Though we may ask ourselves things like, "Should I change the format of this document?" It is not creative thinking—it is judgment. Starting out our day in such a manner can make reverting to a creative mind–set nearly impossible. For this reason, trying to attempt creative thought while at work is generally not considered to be best.

The most appropriate time to formulate ideas is while we are in a relaxed state of mind. There are many activities that foster such an atmosphere like taking a stroll, taking a bath, or sitting in the restroom. For men, even time spent shaving can be good for idea generation.

Nighttime is also suitable for inducing ideas because sleeping replenishes our mental energy. We sometimes have new ideas when we wake up in the middle of the night. To record these ideas I recommend having a pen and paper handy to write them down before they slip the bond of consciousness and return to our dreams. In fact, the importance of writing down ideas can not be emphasized enough regardless of the time frame. When struck with new ideas, we should immediately try to write them down. Writing clarifies the fresh idea and ignites the formulation of associative ideas in turn. Most importantly, as mentioned above, taking notes ensures that our ideas are never lost and prevents them from fading, leaving only the memory of having them behind.

Above all, remember that stimulating the silent area of the brain through mental focus and concentration is the primary ingredient necessary to create optimal conditions for idea generation. Whenever and wherever we best achieve this mental stimulus should be of utmost consideration when tackling the task of generating new ideas.

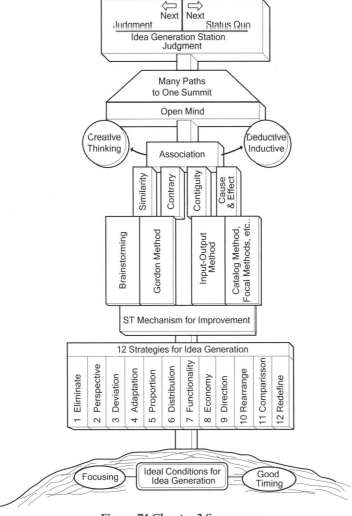

Figure 74 Chapter 3 Summary

Here is a summary chart for approaching idea generation using a plotted, methodical manner.

149

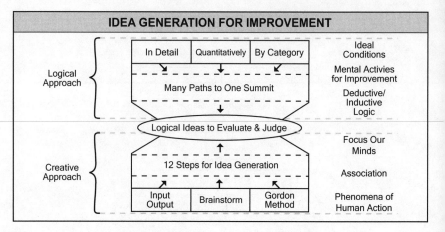

Figure 75 STM Component Chapter 3

The value of this model is to provide ideas that will stand up to evaluation and judgment. As such, the process itself must be rooted in the Logical Approach and combined with the tools highlighted in the Creative Approach. You must have the mental flexibility to realize there is more than one path to reach our goals. Idea generation is a top-down, bottom-up strategic process in which logical and creative methodologies need to be aligned.

IV THE EVOLUTION OF IMPROVEMENT

> Through various experiences, humans have steadily advanced on the path of improvement. Analyzing this history can lend prudent insight as to what direction we should take now to progress further.

Cavemen to Engineers — The Progress of Man and Tools

For prehistoric man the quest for food far outweighed other needs and desires. If we take fruit as an example, it is only logical to assume that more humans meant less fruit. The fruits that remained in the tree tops were well out of the reach of our shorter ancestors. Who knows how long our frustrations simmered until deductive reasoning allowed us to formulate the idea of using tools.

Sticks or steps were used to supplement reach, while stones supplemented raw strength. In all cases, ideas were our source of our power.

Fast-forward fifty million years and we humans can trace our march towards civilization with the development of the tools, machines, and devices we created.

Parallel to the development of machines and other complex tools was the corresponding development of a means to power them. Initially, to conserve their own energy, humans used the power of animals such as horses and cows. Then people harnessed the various forces of nature such as using the power of water, wind power, and gravity. Water mills, wind mills, and the tools that use gravitational force were developed as a result.

However, natural energy sources, while very useful, have limitations. Hydraulic power for instance, can be created only where water is available, and wind power can only be generated when wind is blowing, i.e., there are constraints of space and time. Although gravity is free of space or time constraints, it has directional constraints as it only operates downward.

These drawbacks persuaded humans to seek alternative power sources free from the constraints of space, time, or direction. This eventually led to the invention of steam, gas, and internal-combustion engines. So far, our crowning achievement has been in harnessing electricity, a revolutionary means of power capable of being transmitted across large distances.

In this way, the functionality of our hands and means of power have developed in two directions: *mechanization* and *motorization*. Advancements in factories have happened, and will continue to happen, along these two lines.

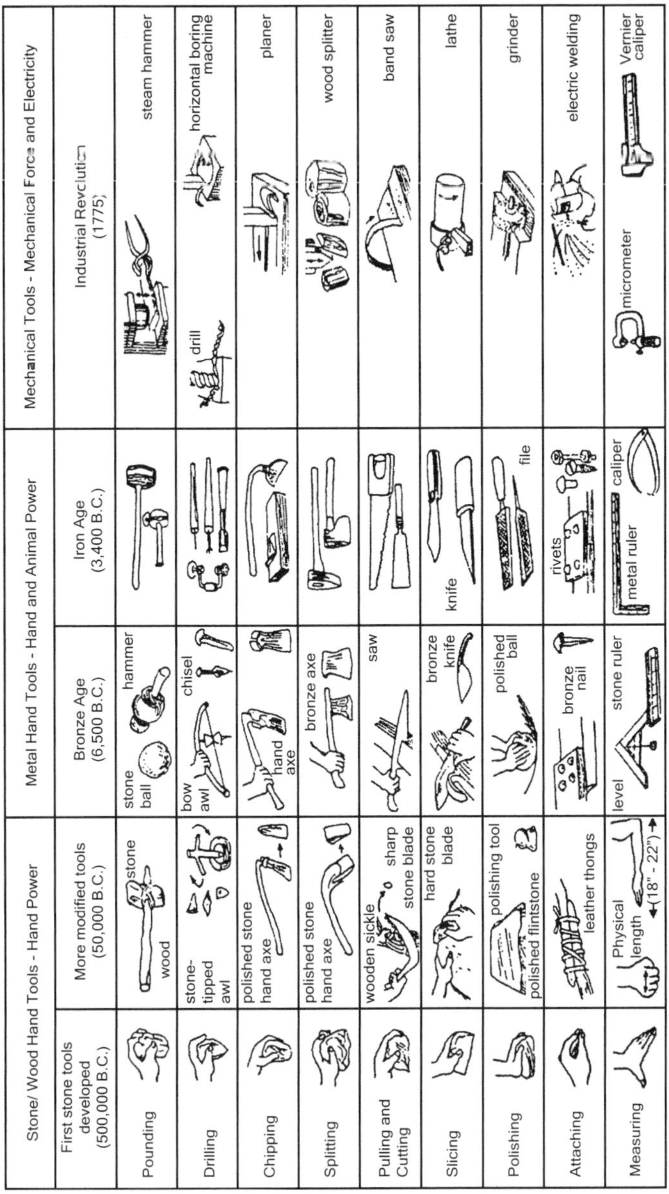

Figure 76 Evolution of Tools

Evolution of tools from prehistory to the start of the Industrial Revolution.

Therefore, when we ask ourselves, "Can a tool or machine replace what my hands are doing now," not only are we generating ideas for improvement, we are also engaged in the process which propels us into our own future.

5 Improvement Principles

1) Mechanization and Motorization

Sterilizing Sausages

One operation at Y Industries, a food manufacturer, consisted of placing sausages in a sterilization chamber. The boiling water in the chamber released heat and humidity and made the work environment difficult to bear. Therefore, the company asked me to mechanize the operation.

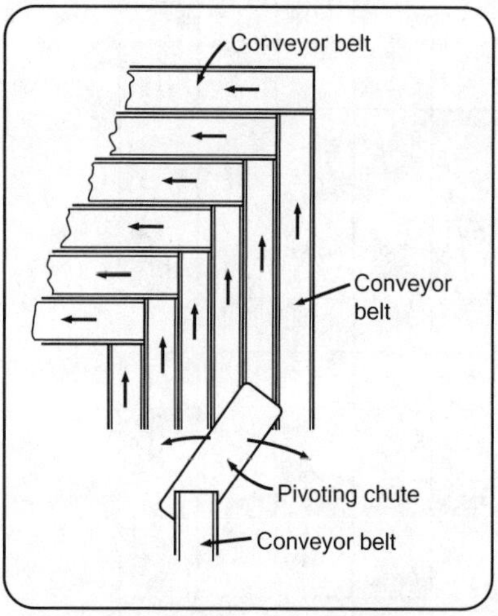

The functionalities required of the machine were as follows:

- Place sausages in the sterilization chamber

- Arrange them in six linear rows

- Place the appropriate number of sausages in an orderly fashion

Figure 77 Conveyor Layout

The task was achieved by using a single conveyer belt that carried horizontally placed sausages, and feeding them into six separate conveyer belts via a pivoting chute (Figure 77).

The sterilization chamber was situated to the left of the belts so I placed six belts laterally that would receive sausages and send them down into the boiling water, all while maintaining their orientation.

Although this idea was good, there was occasionally a problem of sausages dropping from the pivoting chute and landing on top of the retaining walls between the belts. To remedy this I imagined how people would turn the sausages with their hands to fix the orientation. From this visualization I designed the retaining walls with ropes running around them, always in opposing directions (Figure 78).

For example, if a rope on one wall moved upward, a rope on the adjacent wall moved downward. This device worked well and made sausages that fell on top of the retainers drop immediately onto the belts in the correct horizontal direction.

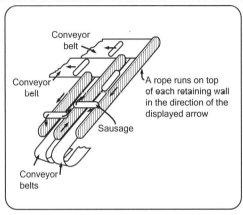

Figure 78 Sausage Retaining Wall

I completed the machine based on the above ideas and did a test run, only to encounter yet another problem. The conveyors and ropes functioned as I intended, but when sausages were dropped into the sterilization chamber, some ended up falling sideways. When this happened the misalignment caused subsequent sausages to stack askew. If left in such an orientation, the sterilization process would result in a rupture or deformation of the product.

To unravel this problem I imagined how workers would place sausages in the

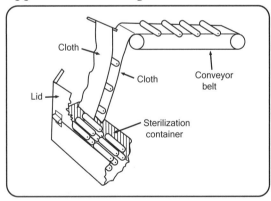

Figure 79 Cloth Sausage Guide

chamber maintaining their proper direction by holding them with their fingers and releasing them near the water. Then I devised a means of incorporating this motion into the machine by draping two thick pieces of cloth at the end of the belts so that the products would roll down between them and fall gently into the water (Figure 79). To my delight, this solution worked brilliantly and finally made the machine complete.

Dynamic Conveyor Guide

On my visit to a food manufacturing plant, I saw a conveyor carrying piles of small fish called croaker. Workers were scraping each pile down to a work table before processing it. This made me wonder, "Why isn't there a mechanism to bring fish down to the table automatically?"

I set to work and designed an arm that would lie across the conveyer belt and guide the fish down a slide and onto the table. However when tested, it did not work as I expected. I did not take into account the fact that the fish were wet from a cleansing process. Because of this, the fish would stick to the conveyor and fail to slide down the ramp.

While I was thinking about how to fix this problem I received a clue by watching a worker next to me quickly grab a pile with both hands and scrape it down to the table. I incorporated the dynamic action of the worker's movement into my design by connecting the arm to a pedal. When the pedal was stepped on, the mechanical arm jostled the fish loose from the belt (Figure 80). This system worked very well; all that was needed was a little jolt.

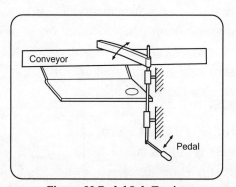

Figure 80 Pedal Jolt Device

This idea of a dynamic guide can also be applied to other products that tend to stick to conveyor belts, such as clay or rubber. By giving a jolt to the guide, through a crank for example, products can easily be removed from the conveyor belt.

Ironing Out Problems

At a foundry that manufactured bases used for clothing irons, one of the operations consisted of removing gates from the castings. Workers would break the gate with a hammer while the casting was still hot. Once the casting cooled, removal was too difficult. As I watched the work, I noticed that the workers were always hitting the gates from a certain angle. After I had that realization, I started wondering if the process could be mechanized. I pitched my idea to the plant president.

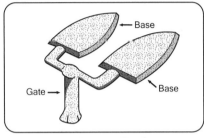

Figure 81 Iron Castings

The foundry bought my idea and introduced a machine as shown in Figure 82. It worked by elevating castings with a conveyor that would drop them from a certain height, whereupon they would strategically strike a board positioned un-

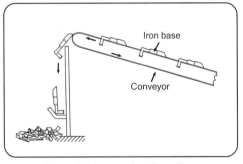

Figure 82 Separating Iron Parts

derneath. The board was angled so that the gates would hit at precisely the same angle that the workers were hitting them with the hammer. The mechanism was a success and freed workers from laborious and dirty work.

Rods in Chutes

Sending rod-shaped items down chutes while maintaining their orientation is a very common challenge at factories.

Sending rods in their longitudinal direction is easy since a semicircular chute is sufficient. The addition of a vibrating

157

motor to this type of chute effectively prevents rods from jamming. On the other hand, sending rods down a chute while it maintains a lateral position is a real challenge. One way to handle this is to use a corrugated chute as shown in Figure 84. Corrugation can also be used in vertical chutes as shown in Figure 85.

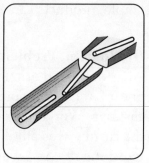

Figure 83 Rod Shaped Items

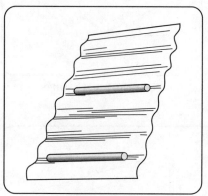

Figure 84 Corrugated Chute

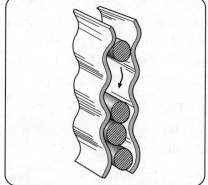

Figure 85 Vertical Corrugated Chute

When this type of vertical chute is used, it is necessary to have a mechanism that releases one rod at a time. Using a device called an "ankle" (Figure 86) is an effective means to achieve this.

- When the ankle tilts downward, it releases the bottom rod while holding the above rods in place.

- When the ankle rotates back up, the stack slides down with the bottom rod held in place by the bottom part of the ankle.

An ankle smoothly transitions a rod from storage by releasing one rod at a time in a controlled fashion. A piston-style dispenser also has the same functionality (Figure 87).

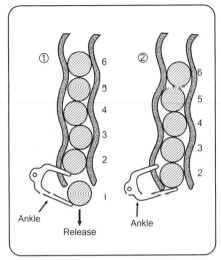

Figure 86 Mechanical Ankle Joint

Both of these dispensers are transformations of hand motions that replaced the need for a worker to take out an item with one hand, while holding the remainder with the other.

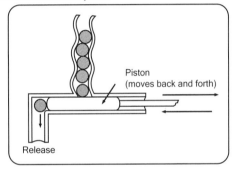

Figure 87 Piston Style Dispenser

Lining Up Metal Parts

One operation at an electric company involved gluing porcelain tubes to metal parts and lining them up on wire mesh. Workers were lining the parts neatly but due to the smallness of the parts, handling was difficult and tiring.

The company thought the operation could be done mechanically especially because the parts were being placed on the mesh with regularity. After some trial and error a relatively simple device that could handle this task was designed (Figure 88). It functioned as follows:

- As the device moves horizontally from right to left, it places 20 parts in one row at even intervals.

159

- When one row is completed, an internal gear moves it vertically.

- Another row is made while it moves from left to right.

Metal parts are being lined up on the left
(Matsushita Electric Industrial Co.,Ltd, Division of Iron)

Figure 88 Alignment Device

This device allowed the parts to be placed neatly in a grid mechanically.

2) The Division of Labor

Division of Labor Benefits	Table 29
• It eliminates unnecessary motions such as picking up a tool and returning it • Repetition makes it easier for workers to focus on given tasks • Work is simplified and the acquisition of skills accelerates • It facilitates the use of tools and machines	

The concept of the division of labor came about over 150 years ago during the Industrial Revolution. As the prevalence of machines grew so did the necessity for people to leave home to work in groups. In order to leverage the range of skills of these groups more effectively the concept of the division of labor was conceived. In needle fabrication for instance, when the operations that a single worker used to perform were divided into 18 tasks and shared among multiple workers, the productivity increased 240 fold.

A closer analysis reveals that the division of labor can be separated into two types: quantitative and qualitative. Quantitative division of labor means that a large task is divided among workers who perform the same operations in parallel. Qualitative division of labor means that a process is divided into elemental operations which are then assigned to workers with the corresponding required skill.

Quantitative division of labor has the following advantages and disadvantages:

Quantitative Division of Labor	Table 30
Advantages	
• It shortens production time	
Disadvantages	
• Many tools and machines are required	
• The quality of the finished products tend to vary	

Qualitative division of labor has the following advantages and disadvantages:

Qualitative Division of Labor	Table 31
Advantages	
• Reduces operations to simple tasks	
• It eliminates unnecessary motions	
• It simplifies work and facilitates the use of tools and machines	
• Skilled workers are easier to find	
• Training of new workers is simpler	
• The operation rates of tools and machines generally improves	
Disadvantages	
• Increases in the number of work areas, increase in traffic	
• Repetition of simple tasks can result in localized fatigue	
• The repetition of simple tasks can create boredom	
• A failure at one operation can spread quickly to other operations	
• Planning and coordinating becomes more difficult	

When implementing the division of labor both advantages and disadvantages need to be taken into consideration. In general, as long as the downsides are dealt with appropriately, the advantages greatly outweigh the disadvantages.

Canning Oranges

For M Canning Factory, the canning industry revolves around seasonal harvests. When fish are in season, the fish are canned, when mandarin oranges are harvested, the oranges are canned. Consequently, the number of employees fluctuates throughout the year and the majority of people on factory floors are temporary workers.

As I talked with the production chief, Mr. Arata, his main concern was a lack of skilled workers. Because of this shortage defect rates were high and conversely, efficiency was low. He said the factory sends buses to apartment complexes in a coal-mining town and hires part-time workers everyday.

While I was on the shop floor, mandarin oranges were being processed prior to canning. Workers first removed the orange stem with a wooden tool and then peeled it. After observing the work for a while I talked with the production chief.

"How many workers do you have here?"

"We have about fifty."

"I have an idea. Why don't you choose ten workers you know to be dexterous and we'll let them remove the stems and the other forty can concentrate on peeling, which doesn't require as much skill."

We tested this arrangement right away, thirty minutes later, the result came in.

- Defects due to damage decreased by 80 percent

- Overall productivity increased by five percent

Most of the damages happened when stems were removed,

so this task was given to relatively skilled workers. The easier task of peeling was assigned to other workers. This division of labor successfully matched the difficulty of tasks with the skill level of the workers. It also simplified each operation and contributed to lowering defects and increasing efficiency.

3) Optimization—Human Functions and Efficiency

The human body is not unlike a machine. For this reason, it is important to provide jobs that match the skill and functionality of this machine. Thus, optimization should be pursued via the following:

- Place workers in jobs that best suit their individual skills

- Consider general human abilities and design jobs accordingly

For the former, using aptitude tests to measure individual skill levels is an effective way to achieve this. To accomplish the latter, the mental and physical functions of humans should be studied and the resulting wisdom used to improve the methodology of the work.

The following is an example of a job successfully redesigned to more closely match the ability of humans. When inspecting high-pressure insulators they

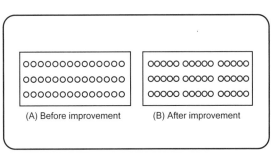

(A) Before improvement　　(B) After improvement

Figure 89 Counting in Fives

were initially arranged in a tray as shown in Figure 89 (A). Workers were supposed to find and remove defects but for some reason they were often overlooked using this arrangement. This result changed when the company modified the procedure to better accommodate human ability.

163

It has been said that the maximum number of items humans can distinguish at once is five. By simply reducing the number of insulators inspected at any given time from a full tray to groupings of five as shown in Figure 89 (B), the company observed marked improvement in their inspection accuracy.

Human physiology and ergonomics should also come into play when redesigning the methodology of work. For example, many factories tend to make their employees work in a standing position, resulting in unnecessary fatigue and producing a negative impact on efficiency. However, allowing workers to sit instead (Figure 90, following page), reduces energy expenditure by roughly 20 percent. If we consider that a standing person would be capable of burning around 1,800 calories a day for manual labor, a sitting worker would therefore use about 350 calories less than a standing worker. This conserved energy could be used to do more work, thereby increasing efficiency. Moreover, by providing adequate and well distributed breaks for workers, efficiency can be boosted even further. Therefore, human psychology and physiology should also be treated as an important consideration when optimizing workplace improvement.

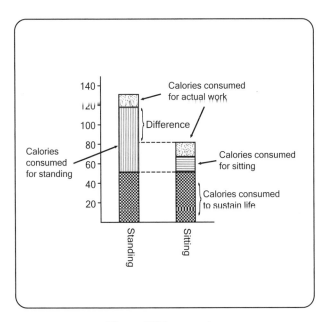

Figure 90 Ergonomics

4) Synchronization — Coordinating the Workforce

As the division of labor evolved, more and more production was completed in series by dividing the work among individuals, eventually resulting in the assembly-line systems we know today. As such, the proper balance of timing and task coordination became more and more important. Inevitably, as more industries such as automobile, home electronics, and food manufacturers transitioned into assembly-line production systems, the need for proper workforce synchronization became unavoidable.

Improperly timed labor leads to frequent delays for workers and machines, causing production efficiency to plummet, inventories to bulge, and corresponding redundancies in transportation to and from storage. Thus, synchronization has become an essential prerequisite for properly managing modern industries.

5) Automation — Mechanizing Judgment

Born out of a desire to mimic human hand functions, machines were eventually endowed with the additional humanistic elements of judgment and adjustment, otherwise known as *feedback functions*. Combining mechanization along with the functionality of feedback is called automation. Even if a machine is technically sophisticated it cannot be considered fully automated without this feedback function.

Feedback is useful not only to machines themselves, but also to those managing them. Regulating the sensitivity and accuracy of the feedback function can have profound effects on production. Thus, managers skilled in analyzing and adjusting feedback accordingly can achieve very favorable results.

I must make clear that these five principles do not represent my thoughts; they are the sum of human experience. However, if these principles are combined with my Scientific Thinking Mechanism it is sure to make turning ideas into reality a successful endeavor.

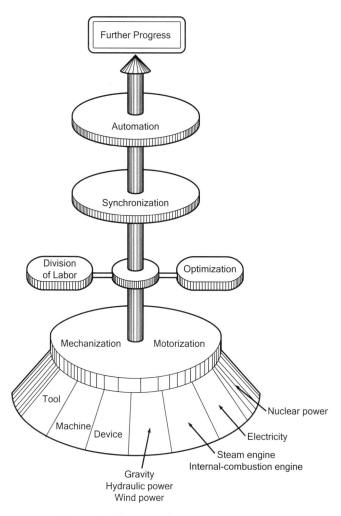

Figure 91 Chapter 4 Summary

Further Progress is inevitable; by using the Five Improvement Principles along with the Scientific Thinking Mechanism, we can suit progress to meet our needs with efficiency and kaizen in mind.

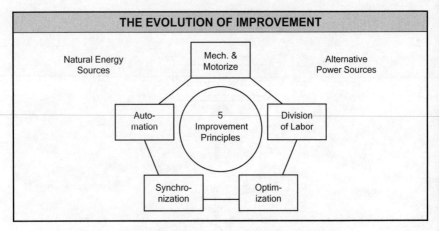

Figure 92 STM Component Chapter 4

The 5 Improvement Principles help us cope with change by teaching us how to direct change. Each principle highlighted in this model explains the process and provides the framework needed to make sound decisions. Since progress is necessary, manufacturing strategies for today's environment need to be flexible enough to mold into tomorrow's.

V FROM IDEAS TO REALITY

> Even the greatest idea can become meaningless in the rush to judgment. To gauge an idea as feasible we must cut our ties to the status quo and find the balance between constructive criticism and judgment. Within that balance we will uncover crucial input for making our ideas a reality.

Separate Idea Generation from Judgment

No sooner do you suggest introducing a flow production system than somebody shoots it down by saying, "Our volume of production is too small to justify that." Or, as soon you have the idea to transport material with a conveyor, you hear that small voice inside your mind say, "No, that just won't work."

These examples are meant to show how a judgmental mindset can destroy an idea before it is even formulated. Nevertheless, judgment remains the primary antagonist in the improvement process, which usually occurs in the following five stages:

Judgment in the 5 Stages of Improvement	Table 32

1. Finding problems—"This looks odd."

2. Idea generation—"How about doing it this way?"

3. Judgment—"It doesn't work in this case."

4. Idea regeneration—"Then, how about this?"

5. Implementation—"Let's do it."

The first stage of finding problems, begins with the premise that the current method of operation is faulty or could be improved. Idea generation follows based on the assumption that this founding premise is valid. Therefore, any ensuing judgment that opposes the ideas generated under this assumption should be considered contradictory to the foundational premise, thus indicating that current operations will remain unchanged.

Improvement usually means doing something that we have never done before. Correspondingly, the whole purpose of idea generation is to formulate solutions that move beyond the status quo, making it an inherently external oriented mental activity. Judgment on the other hand, tends to be a passive and internally oriented mental activity opposed to such action, stemming from our natural fears of change and of the unknown. Obeying the verdict of judgment by default can severely jeopardize progress possibly causing it to escape our grasp on a perpetual basis. However, this in no way implies that we should never pass judgment.

Indeed, in order to encourage positive results, any plan for improvement should be critiqued for feasibility and obvious flaws prior to implementation. But this sort of judgment should be passed from a realistic point of view and only after all ideas have been presented, never both at the same time.

As previously discussed, the popular brainstorming method makes it a rule to shut out criticism during idea generation, exemplifying the fact that in a judgment-free environment, humans can create many great ideas. Conversely, by mixing the two together, we end up extinguishing the fire of creativity that was just ignited, quickly turning it into a pile of smoking ash.

Thus no matter what, judgment and idea generation should be separated. This concept can not be emphasized enough; it is the golden rule to adhere to as we set out on the road to improvement. Like preparing a bath by simultaneously mixing equal amounts of hot and cold water, passing judgment during the creative process will only produce lukewarm solutions at best. Instead, an abundance of hot water should be added first, filling the tub with ideas. Then the coolness of judgment can be used to temper the outcome to perfection.

Overcoming Mental Obstacles

Improvement can be like taking a quiz or reading a mystery novel. As soon as we solve one problem, another one rears its head, followed by another, and yet another. Never ending problems like this can be so overwhelming that, even if the problem we are facing is the last, we often cannot recognize that it is so. Frustrated and demoralized, we tend to seek refuge within the comfort of conventional thought. Yet, most problems do not have a simple conventional solution. Moreover, remaining in such a state of mind sets us up to be snared by our own unconscious judgment. Indeed, saying things like, "There's no way this can be mechanized" serves only to thwart logical improvement efforts, possibly even killing executable plans. These sorts of mental obstacles can be our biggest enemy when tackling improvement; strategies to overcome them can give us just the edge we need to find success and keep us from giving up.

First off, it is always helpful to list all the difficulties before rushing head–first into problem solving. A list makes the blurred outline of problems more understandable by clarifying the relationship between multiple factors and acts as a preemptive measure against unexpected problems that crop up just when you think everything is taken care of.

Once we are in the midst of problem solving we can easily become over-focused and loose objectivity, a condition that can drive us to an impasse. If this happens, leave the preoccupied self behind for a moment and ask questions with an alter ego such as, *What's troubling you?* This method of internal conversation is quite effective at breaking a stalemate and an approach I have used several times to find my way out of difficult situations to reach solutions.

One of the best ways to end a stalemate, like when deadlocked in discussions on improvement, is to just try out an idea. It is said that trial and error is the easiest and most effective means to reach a solution. Besides, an endless cycle of arguments where one inference is pitted against another is a complete waste of time. Whereas the simple act of trying out an idea can provide just the stimulation we need to bring down the wall in our thinking. The following anecdote illustrates this well.

At one factory, a method for improving the operation of a heat-treatment furnace was suggested. Many opposed the idea, saying that groupings of all small or all large parts would not be compatible. Once the new method was tried out, however, it became clear that 80 percent of the groupings had the proper blend of different sized parts, and a way to deal with other 20 percent was also created.

Although a trial like this is important, it does not mean that we should try out our ideas haphazardly. Rather, they should be carried out logically and methodically. For example, when a woman lost her car keys in the sand at the beach she successfully found them in ten minutes by systematically crisscrossing the sand to narrow her search. She would not have found her key nearly as fast if she had just roamed around arbitrarily.

As the above example indicates, formulating our trials or ideas based on the foundation of a logical premise greatly boosts our chances of success. Thus, ensuring that correct logic is used to formulate the premise is very important.

The premise of an improvement idea, and any assumptions that stem from it, are often based on some kind of cause–and–effect relationship supported by varying forms of deductive and inductive reasoning. The following commentary discusses cause, effect, deductive, and inductive reasoning. Quick pointers are provided on what mental pitfalls to avoid when formulating ideas, as well as some advice on ways to measure the validity of our fundamental premise and keep our path to improvement on track.

When thinking about our idea as the cause and the corresponding outcome of that idea as the effect, the logic of our thinking can be verified by asking the following three questions:

Is there really a cause–and–effect relationship?

Is it the *only* cause–and–effect relationship that exists?

Is the cause–and–effect relationship inevitable?   ·

If these three conditions are not satisfied it cannot be said that things have sufficient causal correlation. The three corresponding examples below demonstrate very well a situation where this lack of causal correlation is precisely the case.

There was an assertion that went, "An economic slump makes movie theaters' business sluggish," but it turned out that there was no correlation.

There was an assertion that said, "Economic slumps increase unemployment." In the case of the cotton industry, however, the impact from synthetic fiber was much bigger than the economic condition.

There was an assertion that said, "Sales of electric fans go up in the summer," but the sales were not as robust as expected due to either cold weather or the impact of new air conditioning models.

It goes to show that one should never be too hasty to conclude that a cause–and–effect relationship exists without taking into account these aspects.

When it comes to making assumptions based on our premise, deductive and inductive reasoning are most commonly used. Definitions of both thinking methods are shown below.

Deduction: apply one example to a general situation

Induction: makes a single general theory based on many examples

Although these are proven problem solving methods that humans have been employing for ages, it is important to recognize that they can sometimes be misleading. Here are some examples of illogical decisions based on common misconceptions for each method:

Deduction Method:

After hearing and believing there were no poisonous snakes in Area 1, someone went there only to be bitten by one (quantitative exception).

After hearing that wild mushrooms in the area were edible, someone went and ate some that looked similar to the common mushrooms, only to find that they were poisonous (qualitative exception).

Induction Method:

Deciding that maids these days do not work hard based on the action of just two maids (quantitative insufficiency in examples).

Deciding that the cost of living is much cheaper in Tokyo than in Osaka Although things may look similar from the outside, their overall quality is not (qualitative insufficiency in examples).

A Hole in the Hull

Years ago a strong nor'easter hit hard upon the North Atlantic Ocean. At one port in particular, tall ships were at the mercy of the winds. The ships pitched to and fro like toys in a child's tub and eventually drifted towards the breakwater, despite the captains belief that they were firmly anchored. Skippers and owners gathered at the port to worry and debate over what to do yet no consensus could be reached.

Among those gathered was a young ship owner. During the discussion his ship had drifted toward where they were gathered, pushed by a strong tail wind. Suddenly, he jumped onto his ship and to everyone's surprise made a hole in the ship's bottom with an axe. Water rushed into the ship and it quickly sank two meters to the sea bottom. When the storm had passed, all the other ships were left in splinters, but the young owner was able to raise his ship and repair it.

This story suggests something profound about the attitude we should have when we are faced with problems. It should also serve as a reminder to be wary of common mental obstacles that occur when we:

- Do not evaluate problems correctly
- Lose the courage to face yet another problem
- Cannot bring ideas into action

These are traps many of us fall into when translating ideas into reality. Above all, the best way to fight these challenges is to never give up and know that even if problems cannot be solved completely, improvement is always possible.

Removing Scrap from a Dead-End Hole

At an electric–appliance manufacturer, holes were drilled and then threaded into the shaft of wringers. Afterwards, the external surface of the shaft was polished. However, because the holes did not go all the way through, scrap from the drilling and threading process would get lodged inside only to come out during polishing and scratch the surface. To avoid this workers removed the scrap prior to polishing as follows:

Scrap Removal Process	Table 33
Place shafts inside a basket and immerse it in a bath of soapy water for about 10 minutes	
Shake the basket as it is removed from water	
Hold about 5 shafts at a time and knock the end against a work bench several times to expel the scrap	
Blow in compressed air into the hole to remove remaining scrap	

I happened to walk past a worker doing this last step and asked, "Why do you blow in air?"

"To remove any left over cutting scrap."

"But if you blow air *into* the hole, doesn't it force the scrap farther inside?" I said.

"What should I do instead?" he asked.

"Can you blow air *out* of the hole?"

"No, the hole doesn't go all the way through the shaft."

I thought for a moment at this and then asked, "Can someone go to the infirmary and bring me a syringe?"

"What for?"

"You'll see."

Once I had the syringe, I filled it up with cleaning fluid and affixed a long needle on the end. Then I grabbed a shaft that had just been tapped prior to its immersion in soapy water and inserted the needle of the syringe to the bottom of the hole and squirted the cleaning fluid a couple times. After doing this to ten shafts, I tapped them all lightly against the work bench. No scraps came out. Furthermore, when the outside of the shafts were polished there were no problems with scratching.

This idea was taken a step further through the creation of a machine that cleaned out the scrap while spinning it on a rotor

(Figure 93). Shafts that had been drilled and tapped were placed inside the machine with the hole-side down. A jet of cleaning fluid was injected into the holes as the machine rotated. After the shafts were cleaned they were released automatically. The machine made the entire operation easier and enabled the cutting scrap to be expelled completely.

The cover is removed in the picture to show squirting fluid
(Matsushita Electric Industrial Co.,Ltd, Washing Machine Division)

Figure 93 Cleansing Machine

Although my initial idea was rejected by the worker, I was able to use this input to redirect my thoughts, formulating them into a feasible plan. Thus, instead of halting my idea generation the objection itself became the tool I used to overcome this mental obstacle and achieve success.

Defogging the Water-Level Indicator

When the steam function of an iron was tested at an electric-appliance manufacturer, it was found out that the water-level indicator would fog up easily. Once this happened it was practically impossible to undo.

An electric heating device was used to evaporate the fog, but this method took too long and was by no means something to expect a customer to do. Neither was it structurally possible to

177

clean it by inserting an object such as a cloth or a stick.

While thinking about what could be done, the image of an ant crawling through a narrow pipe came to my mind. I realized then that something that could traverse through small openings, like a gas or a liquid, would have to be used to remove the fog.

Water-level Indicator

Figure 94 Iron

Furthermore, I would have to use a liquid that would not contribute to the condensation. After more thought, I hit upon an idea to use a liquid with a volatile nature. I then added some rubbing alcohol to wash away the inner surface of the indicator and found that it worked quite well and cleared the fog immediately.

Dyeing Yarn

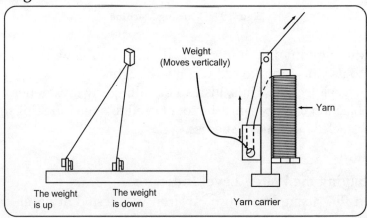

Figure 95 Yarn Braiding Machine

At a textile factory I visited, yarn carriers fed dyed yarn into a machine that then braided it. The carriers kept the yarn at a certain tension by passing the yarn through small weights. The weights were freely suspended and, as such, their height would fluctuate depending on the level of the yarn on the spool. The

178

system worked well except that when the weight was in its lowest position, the yarn often snapped. Whenever this happened, the machine had to be stopped, resulting in unnecessary downtime.

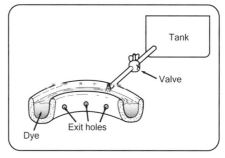

Figure 96 First Improvement

While searching for ways to address this it became clear to me that the dyeing process weakened the yarn. Therefore, I suggested dyeing the yarn after it passed through the weights but before it entered the braider. The mechanism shown in Figure 96 was created based on my suggestion. It included a doughnut-shaped reservoir to hold the dye, a hose fitted with a valve that could control the level of dye flowing from a tank to the reservoir, and small exit holes that allowed dye to ooze out onto the yarn as it passed through.

About a month later I visited the factory and asked how the new mechanism performed.

"It didn't work," said a foreman.

"The yarn didn't dye at all?" I asked.

"Well it did, but it was too uneven to sell as a finished product."

"Uneven? What was the problem?"

"The surface level of the dye wasn't uniform and didn't match the level of the exit holes, causing the dye to seep out unevenly. I guess that could be remedied if we had someone constantly standing by the machine and adjusting the flow with the valve. But of course, that's wasteful."

After thinking about this problem for a while, I suggested using a double-reservoir device as shown in Figure 97. In this setup, 20 percent more dye than was necessary for dyeing would flow continuously into the inner reservoir. Excess dye could

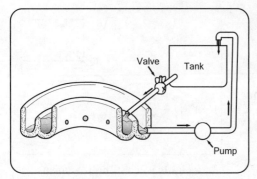

Figure 97 Second Improvement

simply spill over to the outer reservoir and be sent back to the tank by the pump.

I visited the factory about a month later again, and asked how it worked.

"It's no good," said the foreman rather apathetically.

"Dyeing was uneven again?"

"Well, no. That problem disappeared, but now the dye drips excessively out of the holes and onto the braiding machine."

I went to the shop floor and right away saw the problem. It looked like the dripping started due to a request I made upon my last visit. The exit holes were enlarged to exude more dye.

"Now what do I do?" I asked myself as I thought about the precise cause of the dripping. Then I realized that it only happened when the dye was not in contact with the yarn and, therefore, not absorbed immediately. As long as the two were in contact, dripping should not occur. So, I had a groove made around the inner circumference of the cup that connected all the holes (Figure 98). Now the flow of dye was evenly distributed into the groove, ensuring constant contact with the yarn. The problem of dripping stopped completely and finally, my concept was complete.

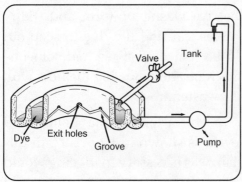

Figure 98 Third Improvement

Just saying that something does not work will never solve a problem. Instead, we

180

need to consider what specific things are preventing it from working and, by maintaining a positive attitude, find ways to overcome those obstacles. This formula was certainly the key to success in this case.

Cooling Oil

At one factory, there was an operation in which piton pins were polished. During the polishing process, a slight dent formed. Although it was as little as one thousandth of a millimeter, it was still undesirable and needed to be addressed. The factory investigated possible causes and found out that a rise in the temperature of the lubricating oil was to blame. When the temperature rose, a bearing inside the machine expanded and caused the problem. Unfortunately, the polishing machine did not have the functionality of adjusting oil temperature.

Someone suggested installing an oil tank underground and connecting it to the machine with a cooling pipe. This would have worked, but was impossible to implement immediately.

I went to the shop floor and checked the structure of the polishing machine. It had a main tank and two subsidiary tanks as shown in Figure 99 on the following page. I thought for a while and then made the following suggestion:

- Place a thermometer in the main oil tank
- Pour oil to its full capacity level, H1

When the temperature rises to a certain level, open valves one and two (V1 and V2), allowing the higher-temperature oil in the main tank to transfer to sub tank two (T2). Once the oil in the main tank is down to the lower level (H2), stop the flow by closing the valves.

Open valve three (V3), allowing regular–temperature oil from sub tank three (T3) to transfer and refill the main tank, thereby adjusting the temperature.

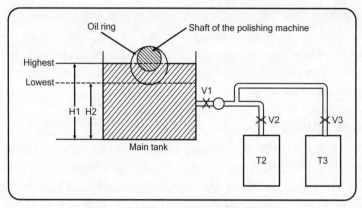

Figure 99 Adjusting Oil Temperature

This method enabled the adjustment of oil temperature without any large investment.

Under Pressure

Y Industries, a well known manufacturer that specialized in metal processing, was planning to introduce a flow production system. However, the cycle time of a particular metal cutting process created a bottleneck and posed a serious problem for achieving one piece flow. While on the shop floor, I observed that a worker at this process would sometimes reverse the blade, remove chips, and apply cutting oil. The time spent for this task was not trivial.

"Why do you reverse the blade," I asked.

"It helps cut the chips in a way that makes them easier to remove."

"Is it possible to cut all the way through without removing the chips?"

"No, the blade will quickly heat up and dull."

"Let's try applying oil as it's being cut." I said and asked him to try. The result, while comical, was not what I had in mind. As soon as the oil hit the blade it went spraying in all directions.

"Oh, this is not good. Please stop!" I cried.

After I asked him to stop and cleaned myself up a little, the issue was still vexing me. While I continued to observe the operation, an idea came to my mind, "How about using pressure to reduce the splatter?" So, we tried shooting the cutting oil at the blade at a higher pressure and in larger volumes. To our surprise, and relief, the splatter was completely suppressed by the pressure.

Whistle Blower

When I went to Taiwan for the first time in 22 years, I visited the factory of S Plastics. During my visit, whistles for use in stuffed animals were being produced, the kind that made noise when the toy was squeezed. The final production process was the sound test. Workers tested the sound of each whistle by actually blowing into them. Considering the sheer number of whistles produced each day, it was a time consuming, and ultimately wasteful, process.

"That seems like a lot of work," I said to one of the workers.

"It sure is. After doing this all day, you don't even want to move your mouth at dinner time."

"Isn't there a way to do it mechanically?"

"We tried several methods, but none that really worked."

"What kind of methods?"

"First, we used a dropper to blow air in, but it was no good. Then we used compressed air, but that didn't work either," he said.

I was actually thinking about suggesting compressed air, so this meant that I was already out of ideas. I pondered my next move.

While I was on the bus to the airport on my way back to Japan, I kept thinking to myself that the air flow had to mimic the workers breath when they tested the whistles by blowing.

So I called the factory from the airport and made a suggestion. "What's needed is air flow that is as stable in pressure and volume as it is when we blow with our mouth. How about conducting a test just using a blower?"

The next week I got a phone call from the factory. The ecstatic person on the other end told me that the blower was a success.

As in all of these examples, if we give up after an initial failure, then success will always elude us. In this case, the failure to create appropriate air flow mechanically was the catalyst that helped focus my thoughts appropriately and find success.

Adhesion of Resin-Coated Fabric

This is a story I heard from Mr. S who attended my Industrial Engineering Seminar held at T Auto Industries.

"Just after I attended your last seminar, I started researching how to adhere resin-coated fabrics electrically. I really wanted to find a way to do it, so I visited Dr. K, a leading researcher in the field of adhesion theory. He said to me, 'There's no way you can do it with electricity,' and explained the reason behind it logically. But I had just learned at the seminar that we should always give an idea a try, so I went ahead and conducted a test anyway. To my amazement, I was able to adhere the fabric. It was an unexpected result even for me, so I called the doctor to let him know of my success."

"Really," I asked, "What did he say?"

"He was astonished; he said 'How odd! Could you bring it over so I could take a look?' The next day I took the fabric sample to Dr. K for him to analyze. Later that afternoon, he called and asked me to come over to his office where he explained to me why electrical adhesion was possible after all. It was a true reminder that you never know what's going to happen unless you try." This is not the sort of experience we encounter often, but facts will trump theory any day of the week; when that happens, good ideas become *great* ideas.

Life vs. Death: The Dichotomy of Judgment

As mentioned earlier, although it is essential to separate judgment from idea generation, it is still an important and necessary part of the improvement process. In light of this, it is helpful to point out the dichotomy of judgment and the power each type has on either making or breaking our improvement plans. The two types of judgment are:

- Positive life bearing judgment

- Negative death bearing judgment

In the case of the earlier yarn–dyeing episode, concluding that the new mechanism would not work just because of uneven dyeing was a death sentence for our improvement efforts. On the other hand, thinking in terms of, "Once the unevenness is corrected," was the attitude that kept our efforts alive.

Depending on which type of judgment we make, the ensuing action and outcome will differ greatly. Those who think, "We can't do it," will likely take no further action. In contrast, those who think, "It'll work if this problem can be solved," will likely act further to find a better method. Naturally, those who make the latter judgment will afford themselves more chances for success.

The profound differences that result from either positive or negative judgment, suggest that the direction we take on our journey to improvement is ultimately contingent upon our attitude.

I have seen cases at many factories where those who are in charge of evaluating improvement ideas end up being the same ones who kill them. We should all take a moment and ask ourselves whether a negative attitude like this applies to us, or to our company.

Engineer's Instinct and Manager's Instinct

At S Electronics, an operation involved hanging parts from

hooks, immersing them in paraffin, and drying them with heat. After the parts came out of the oven, workers were manually removing the parts off the hooks.

As I watched the workers busily removing parts one by one, I talked with Mr. G, the plant manager.

"Isn't there a way to remove the parts mechanically?"

"I don't think that's possible."

"Hmm, I'm not so sure about that. Why don't we place a board underneath the hanging parts and vibrate the parts vertically with a machine?"

I brought a board and gave this idea a try immediately. It resulted in about 30 parts out of 50 coming off, leaving 20 still hanging on the hooks. Mr. G said, "See, it didn't work."

I replied, "What makes you say that? About 30 did come off. Are you saying it didn't work because not everything came off? We can possibly remove 30 this way and remove the rest manually. You have four workers here now, yet you'd only need two doing it this way. You're employing what I call the 'engineer's instinct.' This instinct tells you if something doesn't yield a perfect result, it is a failure. A better instinct would be one that tells you the idea is fine as long as it yields some profit, even if the test results show only 60 percent success. I call it the 'manager's instinct.' If this were a research laboratory the story might be different; but at a working factory, it's ok to go forward with an idea even if it is not perfect. A better–than–nothing mentality is what we need here, not an all–or–nothing mentality."

The factory manager was convinced and took up my idea. I was later told that less than six months after the implementation, the factory improved the method based on their research and succeeded in removing all the parts mechanically.

There was a similar episode that occurred at M Power Company. Audible alarms for pressure switches were inspected. Workers checked the tone of each product by listening to it while enclosed in an insulated chamber. When I asked if it could be done mechanically, I was flatly told that it was technically too difficult for a machine. So instead, I suggested, "How about using a machine to separate the products into three different groups?

- Good

- Defective

- Undeterminable quality

After separating into these groups, workers need only inspect the third group again and determine if these products meet the quality standard or not. Expecting a machine to do the whole inspection may indeed require too much sophistication. But with this method, you don't need a highly sophisticated machine at all." I requested testing this method and left the company.

When I visited the factory again about a month later, I was told that in fact, it was possible to conduct the entire inspection mechanically after all.

This is another example in which people initially balked at improvement efforts due to the apparent lack of perfection, only to find perfection after they set to work thinking that the outcome did not have to be so.

There are types of engineers called "table engineers" who excel in discussion at the table, but hesitate when it comes to actual implementation. This is not the right attitude. As long as a new method provides even the slightest improvement, or profit, we need to be courageous enough to give imperfect methods a try. Furthermore, we must not forget to employ the manager's instinct and judge the situation from a wider perspective, instead of obsessing over technical perfection.

The 10 Objections

Judgment often presents itself in the form of an objection. Furthermore, like idea generation, judgment can also be passed based on an incorrect premise. Therefore, it is important to familiarize ourselves with various kinds of objections so that we can learn to dissect them in order to analyze their validity.

1) Objection Based on Exceptions

I once observed an operation where the lids for stainless steel pots were finished with a machine. Before workers started the operation they marked the machine handle with chalk to indicate where to stop the movement of the machine.

"How about attaching a stopper to the machine so that it stops at the appropriate place by itself?" I said.

"That wouldn't work. There are different sizes of pots, so if I use a stopper, I'll always have to attach and detach it. It'll be less efficient."

Each worker machined 500 lids a day. After thinking about this for a while, I said, "Do you have many pots that aren't a standard size?"

"No, not very many."

"How many, around 100?"

"No, usually only about three or four a day."

It turned out that the irregular-sized pots comprised only a tiny fraction of their workload. With this information alone, we concluded that a stopper could be introduced by simply setting those exceptions aside. Deciding that there is a problem with a suggested idea just because of the existence of exceptions is an illogical argument, yet, one that is used all too often.

2) Nit-Picking Objection

Once I suggested changing a company's payment system from daily-based to performance-based system. People immediately pointed out the disadvantages of this idea one after another:

- It will negatively affect product quality

- It is an unhealthy system that uses monetary incentives to elicit diligence

- It increases labor intensity

On the other hand, they had nothing but good things to say about their current daily-based payment system.

- Income is more stable

- Product quality will not be negatively impacted

This argument gives the impression that the daily-based payment is superior to the performance-based payment in all accounts. But is that truly the case? The reality is every idea that we come up with has both advantages and disadvantages. Pointing out only the disadvantages of newly-suggested ideas is the tactic of "Nit-picking."

We should always use a broad perspective to evaluate both the positive and the negative aspects of both the current and suggested methods. Only then will we be informed enough to conclude which one is indeed a better method.

	Advantage	Disadvantage
Daily-based payment	60%	40%
Performance based payment	75%	25%

Figure 100 Pay System Differences

3) Unit Manipulation Objection

Even if the same phenomenon is described, varying our phrasing or our numerical units can profoundly alter the impression of the listener. Correspondingly, we should be aware that such tactics can, and often are, used to manipulate the listeners' interpretation.

But first, let us take a look at the following expressions:

Production time was reduced from five to four minutes

Production time was reduced by one minute

Production time was reduced by 20 percent

Production increased by 25 percent

24 more products can be produced per day

672 more products per month and 8,064 products per year can be produced

All of the above describe the same phenomenon, yet each version sounds different to listeners' ears.

Here is another example:

"This chicken croquette tastes funny. Does it contain something other than just chicken?"

"Why yes, it does."

"What is it?"

"Oh, there's a little bit of horse meat mixed in."

"Horse meat!? Just how much horse meat is a "little bit?""

"About a 1:1 ratio."

"What do you mean by a 1:1 ratio?"

"There's one chicken used per horse."

4) Objection Based on Incomplete Evidence

Making decisions without first reading the fine print will mean paying high costs later. A classified ad in the newspaper said, "Monthly payment: $245," in big letters. But the fine print on the side said, "Basic payment is $45. There is a $200 bonus rewarded to those who achieve their target."

Similarly, I have seen advertisements claiming that their "spot welder uses 30 percent less energy." I cannot help but wonder how the comparison is measured. It is akin to saying, "My brother is three years younger, and I am three years older." We may conclude that a comparison is being made between the two brothers, but a closer inspection reveals that this is really not clear at all.

People sometimes start their argument with, "According to Hegel," or "According to Dr. . . . ," assuming that what the luminaries have said is the absolute truth. However, unless we take into consideration the details directing these assumptions, we can easily become trapped in a false argument with no real evidence to support our claims.

5) Out-of-Context Objection

At Company B a year-end wage dispute was in progress between labor and management. The labor union was demanding an additional $400 per pay period. After negotiations, management offered $350. One radical union leader returned to the union members and called out to the crowd, "The Company rejected our demand. I say we go on strike."

When the prevailing mood of the members was leaning toward a strike, one member inquired, "Did management make any kind of offer?" The union leader finally revealed that they did and that it was $350. At this, the atmosphere of the room changed completely. Most of the people thought this was a reasonable middle ground. As a result of this crucial information, both sides reached an agreement and the strike was averted.

If the union leader had said, "Management offered only $350 and rejected our demand. I say we go on strike," people would not have been misguided. It goes to show how easy it is for context to be lost when we filter quoted information out of convenience or to serve our own agenda.

This is especially problematic if the original remark has a subjunctive tone, i.e., an "if" sentence. For example, assume that the original remark was, "If steel price goes down by 10 percent, export of ships will increase by 30 percent." Taking this out of the context by reporting, "A 30 percent increase in ship export was announced," could lead to a grave misunderstanding.

6) Chicken-or-Egg Objection

The chicken can only come from an egg; the egg can only come from a chicken. But which on earth comes first? Although I have heard that evolutionary theory explains that the egg comes first, it is indeed hard to make sense of it. The more you think about it, the question just goes around in circles. There is a style of objections similar to this.

"A power shortage was caused because coal was in short supply."

"Coal was in short supply because of the power shortage."

Another example:

"People earn more if they work hard."

"People work hard if they earn more."

These are typical chicken–or–egg objections. If the discussion starts to go in circles in this manner it is better to cut it off and review the topic from a different angle.

7) Tadpole Objection

Everyone knows that tadpoles eventually grow into frogs. However, tadpoles are still tadpoles and cannot be compared to frogs on an equal footing. Sometimes during a discussion, two reference points are likewise compared as equivalent while changes that may have occurred over time are ignored.

For example, a man from Tokyo came to visit me in Kyushu, the southernmost island of Japan, and said, "I thought it would be warmer here than in Tokyo, but it's not."

"When did you leave Tokyo?" I asked.

He said he had left Tokyo a week before and stopped in Nagoya and Osaka on the way. He was unwittingly comparing the previous week's temperature of Tokyo with Kyushu's temperature that day.

The tadpole objection often appears soon after a new method is implemented on the shop floor. In response to the change, workers might start claiming, "The previous method was much easier; this new method is too difficult." But it is unfair if they are comparing the level of comfort they had with a method they used for the past seven years, for example, to the new method they have only used for a week. It is an invalid 'tadpole objection.'

8) Cross-Eyed Objection

Among different opposing objections, the cross-eyed objection is seemingly the all-around favorite. Using this argument, one can sound like they are all for improvement, just not the one you might be suggesting. It is designed to protect the status quo.

At a plant I visited, I saw a worker carrying heavy boxes from the workbench to the product storage area.

I said to the foreman who was with me, "Why don't you place a slide between the workbench and the storage area and move the boxes by simply sliding on it?"

"I actually thought about it, but it would block the aisle where people and carts have to go through. So we can't do that."

Faced with a seemingly logical opposition, I was tempted to say, "Oh, it's an aisle there. I guess there's just no way to change the current method," but I did not.

The points of my suggestion and the foreman's opposition were as follows:

- Goal — facilitate transportation of boxes

- Means — install a slide

- Objection — the installed slide would block the aisle

In other words, his objection was not denying the goal at all. In fact, his objection was only pointing out a flaw in the means to achieve the goal. His opposition, however, was phrased in a way that suggested the goal was not achievable. This style of objection is called a cross-eyed argument.

There are always multiple means to reach a single goal. In this case, just because a slide would inconvenience the overall workplace was not a reason for obliterating the entire idea for

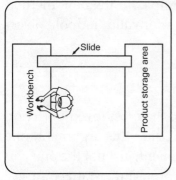

Figure 101 Fixed Slide

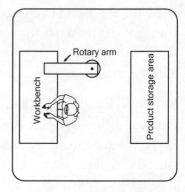

Figure 102 Rotary Arm

improvement. We just needed to devise a different method that could move the boxes without blocking the aisle. There were several ways to achieve this, such as using a rotary arm as shown in Figure 102, or using a suspension mechanism attached to the ceiling.

Here is another example of a cross–eyed objection that occurred during a visit to a tobacco plant. While on the shop floor, I walked by workers wrapping up rolling tobacco. As shown in Figure 103, a conveyor belt was located in front of the workbench. The steps of the operation were 1) wrap the tobacco one pack at a time, 2) when four packs are wrapped, hold them and

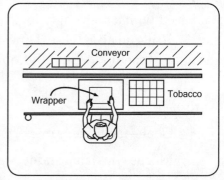

Figure 103 Tobacco Assembly Station

extend the arms all the way to the conveyor and place them on the belt.

I said to the foreman, "Why don't we install a chute that runs between the workbench and the conveyor belt and send the packs one by one after they're wrapped?"

He turned this down at once. "Unfortunately, that wouldn't work. If you slide the packs immediately after they are wrapped,

194

the adhesive won't hold."

"The adhesive won't hold . . ." I was disappointed. As I thought more about it, I realized it was a clear case of a cross-eyed objection.

The goal of my suggestion was to improve the following undesirable aspects of the operation:

- The workers constantly had to keep track of the number of packs wrapped.

- Every four packs, the rhythm of their wrapping motion was disrupted.

- The conveyor belt was too far and caused fatigue to the workers.

On close examination, the foreman's objection—the glue would not hold—only pointed out the flaw of the means suggested, not a single aspect of the purpose above. Yet his response was still, "It wouldn't work." It was a case of cross-eyed argument where the objection makes it sound like the whole purpose was faulty, even though it actually only referred to the suggested means.

Once I realized this I thought that the goal could still be achieved, so long as we made sure the glue did not come loose. I looked into how long it took for the glue to be dry enough so that the packs could be safely slid down the chute. It was roughly equivalent to the time it took to wrap five packs.

So, I had a chute set up to the left of each worker (Figure 104). It was placed strategically so that if a worker simply placed packs on the workbench side by side, the

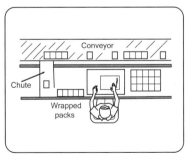

Figure 104 Assembly Station with Chute

sixth pack, the oldest pack at the end of the line, would slide down the chute. This method addressed the flaw of the previous means the foreman pointed out, while simultaneously achieving my goal.

9) Rotary Objection

I went to see the movie *Shiroi Sanmyaku* (White Mountain) with my friend, Y. On our way back he said, "That was a great movie, wasn't it? I was really impressed."

"You really think so? I was disappointed."

"Why? I thought it was great." Our argument went on like this for a while. When we got to the corner where we had to part ways, he asked me, "So what was it about the movie that you found boring?"

I said, "The movie is touted as a documentary, but I've heard that the mother bear isn't even real. Do you remember the scene where the eagle swooped down and flew away with the cub? That was just ridiculous. I think it's distasteful for a documentary to be manipulated like that."

"I completely agree with you there," he said.

"What? So you thought it was distasteful too? Then what was it that impressed you?"

"I was referring to the beauty of the Japanese Alps throughout the year and the brilliant colors of nature. Above all, for the amount of effort the camera crew put in to making the movie possible, I think it deserves respect."

"Now, that I agree with completely," I said. In the end it seemed we actually had the same view on the movie from the very beginning.

So how could we go on arguing without noticing this? Even though we were talking about the same movie, we did not clarify which aspect of it we were referring to specifically.

I was at a meeting once where the topic of discussion was the improvement of productivity. People seemed to be talking past each other so I asked what aspect of improvement each person was talking about in particular. One said he was talking about increasing productivity through intensifying labor, while another said she was talking about increasing productivity through eliminating waste. The same general topic, but distinctively different aspects of it were being discussed on the same table. It was only natural that the discussion was going around in circles.

10) Evasive Objection

Even though his main duty was to supervise the shop floor, the foreman at one company was spending almost an hour a day writing up complicated work reports.

The task was time consuming for him because the content of the reports mainly pertained to accounting, an area outside his expertise. To allot him more time to concentrate on his main duties, I asked to modify the reporting process so that the foreman only had to submit a simple report. At that point, cost accountants could do the rest of the accounting–related work.

I went to visit the accounting manager to sell this idea.

"I want to simplify the reporting from the shop floor and use this format: one sheet per one type of product."

"Let me see…," he looked at the form and said, "If we're to use this form, we'll need more personnel."

"Yes, I'm aware of that. The shop floor agreed to assign five clerks to the accounting department."

He continued without responding to my answer.

"This will require a lot more paper."

"I already got approval from the department chief on that."

"I don't think we have any extra room to accommodate new people."

"How about using one of the conference rooms that general affairs have?"

No sooner had I finished my sentence than he said, "How

about desks?"

"We can bring them from the shop floor."

He kept changing subjects, one after another without responding to any of my remarks. We kept going back and forth, both of us tiring quickly. Eventually, the argument returned to a topic we had already discussed. He then eyed his watch and said, "I have a meeting to attend," and left.

Hear Objections Out

No matter what kind of argument we find ourselves in we should always avoid countering one objection with another. This will only lead to a heated dispute, not to a solution. Rather, it is important to absorb the criticism by saying, "You have a point," or "Right, I didn't think about that." This will give the other party certain psychological satisfaction and make them more receptive to your idea.

In case of the Evasive Argument above, it is especially important to acknowledge the other person's objection first by saying, "Right, we need to think about personnel," or "Yes, I have to take into account the amount of paper it requires." You can start arguing your case after making sure that every objection has been voiced.

There is a saying, "Humans tell the truth, but it only represents one aspect of the truth, not the whole truth." Objections often reveal the inadequacies of our ideas. As such, it is important to be sensitive when raising an objection and do so in the form of advice, not flat denial.

99 Percent of Objections are Advice

After covering the separation and timing of judgment, we also discussed how judgment comes in forms of objections. However, by changing our word choice or our frame of mind, objections can actually be considered cautionary advice. Even though they appear to be objections, judgments of this kind are often directed only at the suggested means, or how the means should be applied, not to the purpose of the proposed idea.

Take the earlier example of wrapping packs of tobacco. The phrase the foreman used in response to my idea was, "It won't work because the adhesive won't hold." But, compare that to this hypothetical response, "That's a good idea, but the adhesive might not hold." Notice that they are essentially conveying the same message, only phrased differently. Looking at it in this light we can see that objections are by nature, advice. Indeed, if I had not adjusted my perspective to see things this way and pressed forward with my original idea in spite of the foreman's objection, I would have surely failed. This is an *extremely important* concept to embrace when pursing improvement. In doing so, what was a seemingly blatant mindset disappears. Arguments then become a simple exchange of facts (although they often represent only one aspect of the fact, not the whole), making discussions of any sort smoother and more relaxed.

Throughout the examples I have shown and countless other occasions not recorded in this text, using the concept of changing objections to advice has proved to be an infallible tool for achieving successful improvement. Granted there is a small portion, say 1%, that might be based on misunderstandings or deliberate ill will. On the basis of my experience, I contend that the remaining 99% of objections in the world are indeed advice. Whether or not they appear as such depends entirely on the words chosen to convey them. Whether or not they are perceived as such depends entirely on you.

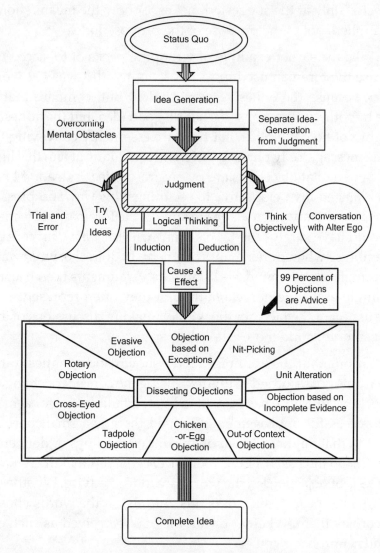

Figure 105 Chapter 5 Summary

Turning ideas into reality always starts with questioning the status quo. As you can see, dissecting objections and taking them as advice is the last stage before having a complete, unique idea.

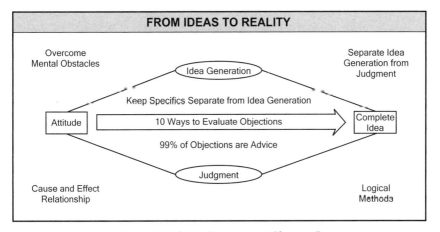

Figure 106 STM Component Chapter 5

Judgment needs to be separated from idea generation. All of our efforts are pointless unless we are committed to this; if not, a complete idea will never be generated. Having the right attitude during idea generation and judgment sets the atmosphere to properly evaluate numerous ideas, as well as objections. Properly used, this model converges attitude and evaluation into an organic whole that will help you produce a complete idea.

VI PROMOTING IMPROVEMENT IDEAS

> If improvement ideas are never realized, plant improvement will never come to pass. In many cases, ideas are implemented not by you, but by someone else.

Cultivating an Appetite for Change

When the time comes to promote and sell improvement ideas, the biggest obstacle will be overcoming the objections of people who think the current methodology of work is satisfactory. Of course, if the party you are pitching your idea to is already unsatisfied with the current situation, they will be open to and interested in new suggestions. However, the reality is that nine out of ten people believe that the current method of operation does not present any inconvenience. If asked what they think about their current method, these people might say, "We may have issues that need to be addressed," but only because they believe that is the expected response. To win over these skeptics it is quite helpful to use detailed analysis and quantitative measurements that can unequivocally demonstrate that their status quo has, in fact, much room for improvement.

For example, at one company the foreman at the shop floor was reluctant to accept my suggestion of improving a machine's operation rate. I had him observe the machine and record how it was used at regular intervals. His own results made him realize that the operation rate was much lower than he expected. From that point on he became an avid proponent of improvement. It goes to show that just having a good idea is not enough for it to be accepted. Therefore, the first and most important step of idea promotion is to prime the receptiveness of others by cultivating their appetite for change.

90-Point Policy

I met with Mr. Tsuji, the efficiency manager of R Electric Company. He said, "I adhere to what I call a '90-point policy.' What I do is, even if I have a perfect idea—a 100 point idea, in other words—I intentionally make it imperfect and present it as a 90-point idea. That way, the person who is listening to my suggestion can point out its faults. Then, I incorporate what was pointed out and make it perfect.

"Since I started this style of suggestion, the time it takes to reach an agreement and actual implementation of the idea has become much shorter. It's probably because those in charge feel that their opinions not only benefit the initial idea, but also contributed to the overall improvement."

In truth, it is a fascinating way to approach objections; to me it is similar to people's perception of other people. Beautiful women are often considered to be cold and unapproachable, while those with some flaws tend to attract more friends.

Here is another episode showing people's propensity to point out flaws. Mr. T, the chief of a municipal office, expressed his slight objections by the way he pressed his stamp of approval. If there was a plan voted on while he was away, or whenever he felt critical about something, he would turn his stamp 90 degrees, signifying that the suggestions have some flaws just not enough for him to disapprove. Some of us may criticize or laugh at this behavior as being arrogant, but this seems to me to be natural reflection of human mentality. I believe that there is a part in everyone's mind that is somewhat arrogant or proud, and desires to point out shortcomings of new propositions. Therefore, those who suggest new ideas need to understand this mentality and handle it wisely.

Understanding and Persuasion

Just because a theory has been explained and understood by people is no guarantee that they will act on it. Indeed, people often will not take action unless they have been persuaded.

It is said that persuasion is achieved not by reason, but through emotions. It is not rare for people to think, "I think what he's saying is right. But I won't do it because I don't like him."

To get people to carry out your idea it is not enough to explain your idea logically. You must put yourself in their shoes and respect their point of view.

All humans feel delighted when others agree with their ideas. Older people talk about the past and console one another or toot their own horns about the fish they caught the other day even though no one was asking. These actions are just manifestations of this aspect of human psychology. For this reason during discussions, it is extremely important to sincerely lend an ear to what other people are saying.

As mentioned earlier, when the opinions of others are different from yours, their disagreement is directed at the means, not the purpose. And there are always multiple means to a reach a single end. In essence this implies that there will always be a means both parties can agree upon. If we understand this and remember to respect the views of other people persuasion will be achieved much easier, and along with it, the realization of our ideas.

Beware the Force of Habit

Animal Experiment on Habit

The following experiment was conducted on four different animal species: a chimpanzee, a dog, a chicken, and a human child; the research was to analyze the ability of each animal to overcome an induced habitual eating behavior. First, to induce the behavior pattern, the animal was put in a cage and everyday food was placed in the same location in front of iron bars that afforded the animal space enough to access the food. This continued for a while until the animal became accustomed to the procedure. Then the food was placed a little farther, just outside of its reach and the back door was opened (Figure 107). The criterion for measuring the process was the time it took for the subject to recognize the open door and to utilize that information to modify their behavior.

Figure 107 Learned Behaviors

When the test was first conducted on the chimpanzee, the animal first made attempts to reach the food by extending its arms through the bars as far as it could. It repeated the same action for some time without success. Eventually however, the chimpanzee noticed that the back door was open, left the cage from there and obtained the food successfully. When the same experiment was conducted with a dog, the canine found the food in no time.

When the experiment was repeated with a five-year-old child, the time the child took to reach the food was shorter than the chimpanzee but longer than the dog.*

When a chicken was put in the cage, however, it was never able to overcome its habitual behavior and, as such, never found a way to reach the food.

It is truly frustrating if new ideas have to be pitched to people with the same adaptability as the chicken.

"How about trying this method?"

"No, I think the current method is better."

"But it'll be much easier this way, since we don't have to carry heavy items."

"Listen to me, I don't want to change, and to be honest, your suggestions are getting under my skin!"

Those who stubbornly cling to the established method, like the chicken, may never be able to reach the appetizing reward of improvement.

True Value of Improvement

In a simple experiment, the time taken to complete a task under two different writing systems was measured in 20 consecutive sessions. First the researchers began with an existing system followed by a new system. Data from these sessions were plotted as completion time over session number, such that the learning curve associated with the adoption of a new system could be compared to that of an existing one.

In the first 20 sessions, participants were instructed to write the name "Ninomiya Kinjiro" in katakana. The results of these tests revealed that participants could consistently write the words at a relatively fast pace. In the next 20 sessions, partici-

---

*Of course, dogs can smell odors at concentrations one million times smaller than we humans can.

pants were asked to write the same word while skipping every other syllable, thus spelling "Nimikijio." In contrast to the original system, the completion time using this new writing system was significantly longer during the first few sessions. However, aside from a small spike re-

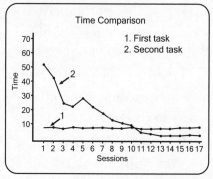

Figure 108 Time Comparison

sulting from participants' hesitation with their spelling, the time to complete tasks under this new system dropped sharply over the course of 13 sessions. Eventually the participants could consistently complete the task in half the time as with the original system.

Halving the number of syllables in a writing task, as in the second system above, can be considered an improvement in cases where the text length needs to be short, like in telegrams. We need to be aware of the fact that, until people become completely confident with what they are doing, such a change can initially hamper productivity. Therefore, the real benefit of an improvement may not be apparent unless those applying it are given ample time to adjust to the new method. All too often people conclude that a previous method was easier before giving a new one the chance to mature to its full potential. This kind of hasty decision nips the improvement in the bud, killing what could have been very successful plan, if only it had been nurtured a little more.

Often times our logic for such decisions is skewed by a force of habit that tells us an existing method as easier. While the methods we are already accustomed to may seem the easiest, they are not necessarily the best. Desperate adherence to this kind of mentality can greatly impede improvement efforts and must be overcome. To do so we have to remain vigilant in our efforts to win over the support of others through persuasion and understanding.

Fear of the Unknown

When faced with the unknown, however small the task, we almost inevitably become conservative. This phenomenon is especially pertinent to improvement ideas because by their very nature they are things that have never been tried.

I often hear people conservatively say, "I'll try it if a good outcome is guaranteed." Yet, I cannot help but wonder how it is possible to know a result without even trying. It is the same as saying, "I won't swim until I'm able to swim." Those who say it will certainly never drown, but they will also never learn how to swim either.

As long as the improvement idea is well planned we should be courageous enough to give it a try, even if elements of it seem less than perfect. Such boldness can often be the only difference between success and failure. Take the following behavioral experiment involving a leopard and a human child.

The experiment analyzed the food acquisition behavior of each subject under two conditions. In the first condition, food was placed in the center of a spiral shaped cage, while the subject was placed at the entrance of the spiral. For the second condition, the positions of food and subject were reversed. In both experiments the subjects had to navigate their way through the cage to reach the food. Interestingly, the results of the experiment revealed distinct differences in the behavioral responses of the two species.

In the case of the leopard, the animal could successfully reach the food when it was placed in the center of the spiral by tracking down its steadily increasing smell as it walked inward. However, in the reverse condition the leopard would stop in the middle, unable to reach the food, presumably because there were certain turns in the spiral where the animal had to walk *away* from the smell.

In contrast the human child could reach the food in both settings without any problems. In other words, a human could foresee what the current action would lead to in the near future even if it meant a temporary deviation from what may have smelled like the correct course.

Quantitative Estimate

This experiment reveals an important distinction between humans and other animals in that we have the wisdom to plan for the future and act based upon this plan, even if the action seems detrimental in the short term. Nevertheless, as I have been pointing out, humans often resist changes for reasons such as habit or fear. If the people you are trying to promote your ideas to are inclined to resist change, the following are effective ways to defuse their concerns:

Present a simple demonstration showing the key features of the improvement idea

Present a concise quantitative estimate of the necessary investment costs and corresponding return and other benefits of implementation

Presenting an idea visually in this manner is a powerful tool we can use to provide people a sense of security. It takes the abstract and gives it a shape that people can relate to, thus easing their fear of the unknown. In turn, you can use that sense of security to harness the power of improvement and blast through the wall of the status quo like dynamite.

Looking in the Mirror

Various methods for promoting our improvement ideas to others have been discussed in this chapter. However, in many cases, it is actually our own self that requires the most convincing. "How about doing it this way? No, that will pose a problem in this case." Have we not all experienced scrapping our own ideas this way?

Six Bananas

When implementing an improvement idea, the act of implementation and its ensuing benefits have to be considered separately.

As long as the purpose of improvement is correct more than likely we can overcome opposition and implement the idea. However, deciding how to distribute the benefits resulting from implementation is a different story altogether.

The following notes highlight an interesting experiment performed regarding this issue. Two monkeys that are cooperative in nature and another two that are aggressive in nature, were used for this experiment. At a given time, two monkeys were placed in a cage along with six bananas.

When the two cooperative monkeys were placed in a cage, both monkeys got three bananas each.

When a cooperative monkey and an aggressive monkey were paired, the aggressive one got all six bananas.

When the two aggressive monkeys were paired, each got only one banana and kicked the remaining four out of the cage.

How does this reflect on our own behavior . . .?

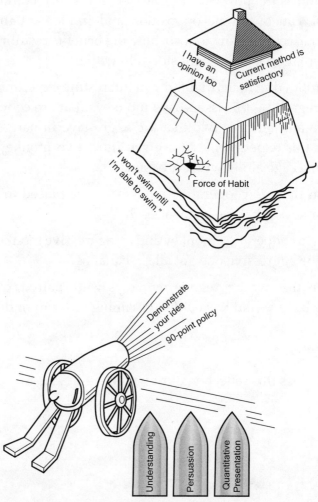

Figure 109 Chapter 6 Summary

The best weapon against the bastion of the status quo lies in persuasion through a quantitative presentation of facts, and a psychological understanding of why people object to new ideas.

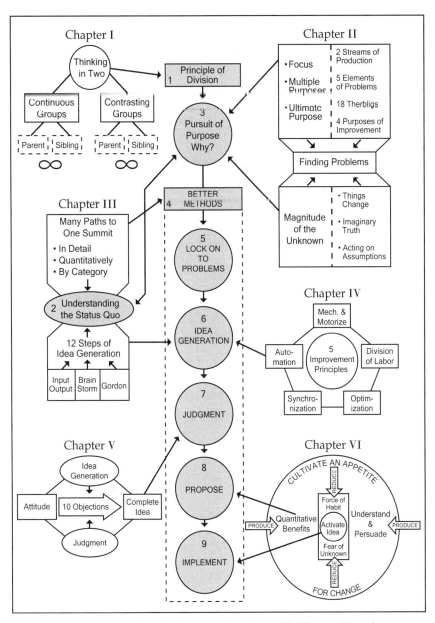

Figure 110 Scientific Thinking Mechanism with Chapter Notations

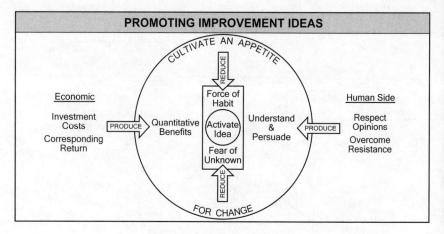

Figure 111 STM Component Chapter 6

The end result of the Scientific Thinking Mechanism is to have a pre-qualified idea ready to activate. When promoting your improvement ideas be prepared to appeal to the human side and economic considerations of improvement. As demonstrated in this model, efforts need to be focused in order to cultivate an appetite for change while reducing natural human fears and habits. Idea generation is a continuous process and a great idea of today is the status quo of tomorrow.

SCIENTIFIC THINKING MECHANISM COMPONENTS
BY CHAPTER

Chapter One

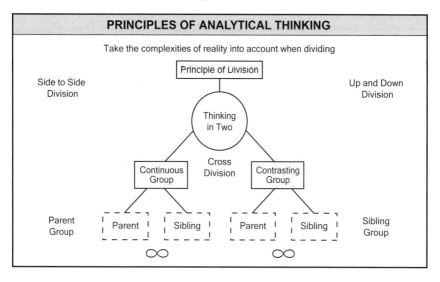

CHAPTER TWO

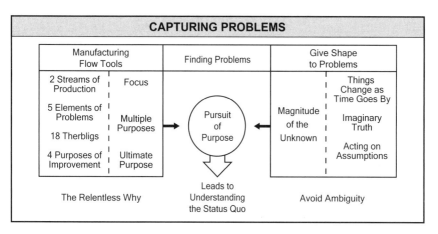

Chapter Three

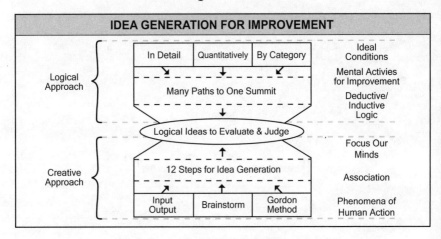

IDEA GENERATION FOR IMPROVEMENT

Logical Approach	In Detail	Quantitatively	By Category
	Many Paths to One Summit		

Logical Ideas to Evaluate & Judge

Creative Approach	12 Steps for Idea Generation		
	Input Output	Brainstorm	Gordon Method

Ideal Conditions

Mental Activies for Improvement

Deductive/ Inductive Logic

Focus Our Minds

Association

Phenomena of Human Action

Chapter Four

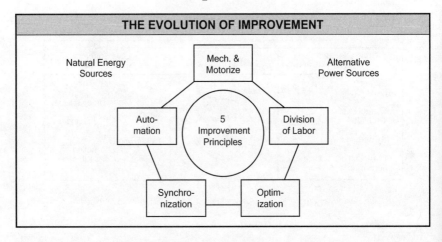

THE EVOLUTION OF IMPROVEMENT

Natural Energy Sources

Alternative Power Sources

Mech. & Motorize

Auto-mation

5 Improvement Principles

Division of Labor

Synchro-nization

Optim-ization

216

Chapter Five

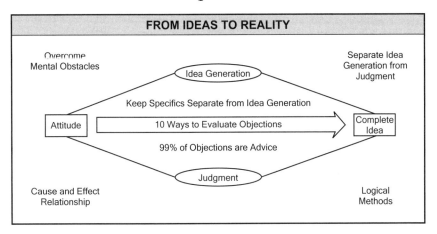

FROM IDEAS TO REALITY

Overcome Mental Obstacles

Separate Idea Generation from Judgment

Idea Generation

Keep Specifics Separate from Idea Generation

Attitude

10 Ways to Evaluate Objections

Complete Idea

99% of Objections are Advice

Judgment

Cause and Effect Relationship

Logical Methods

Chapter Six

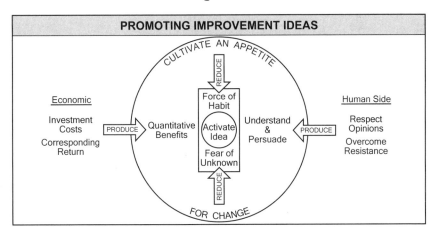

PROMOTING IMPROVEMENT IDEAS

CULTIVATE AN APPETITE

REDUCE

Economic

Investment Costs

PRODUCE

Quantitative Benefits

Force of Habit

Activate Idea

Fear of Unknown

Understand & Persuade

PRODUCE

Human Side

Respect Opinions

Overcome Resistance

Corresponding Return

REDUCE

FOR CHANGE

Short Biography of Shigeo Shingo

1909	Born in Saga City, Japan

1924	While pursuing studies at Saga Technical High School, Shigeo reads Toshiro Ikeda's *The Secret of Eliminating Unprofitable Activities*.

1930	After graduating with a degree in Mechanical Engineering from Yamanashi Technical College, he is employed by Taipei Railway Factory.

1931	Works as an engineer in the casting shop at the Taipei Railway Factory and sees the need for process improvement while there. Realizes the need for rational plant management after reading accounts of the streamlining of operations at Japan National Railways plants. Reads and studies many books, including Taylor's *The Principles of Scientific Management*, the works of Yoichi Ueno, and texts published by the Japan Industrial Association.

1937	Becomes thoroughly instructed in the "motion mind" concept of Ken'ichi Horikome during the first, two month Long-Term Industrial Engineering Training Course in September. This is sponsored by the Japan Industrial Association.

1943	On orders from the Ministry of Munitions, transfers to the Amano Manufacturing Plant (Yokohama) to work as Manufacturing Section Chief. While there he raises productivity by 100% by applying flow operations to the processing of depth mechanisms for air launched torpedoes.
1945	After his success at Amano Manufacturing, the Ministry of Munitions once again transfers him to another maker of similar air-launched torpedo depth mechanisms. He achieves the same results. Moves to Takanabe-cho in Miyazaki Prefecture after accepting a post at Yasui Kogyo (Kita Kyushu) starting in April 1946. He is introduced to the Chairman of the Japan Management Association during a visit to Isamu Fukuda in Tokyo. Here he is asked to participate, on a temporary basis, in an investigation to improve operations at the Hitachi vehicle manufacturing facility at Kasado. After the temporary investigation is over, he is asked to join the service of the Japan Management Association.
1946	Comes to his first revolutionary idea when he concludes that processes and operations are inseparable while waiting for cranes during process analysis at Hitachi. Reports his findings at a Japan Management Association technical conference. While studying the layout of Hitachi, Ltd. Woodworking plant he devises a method of classifying like operations by counting non-interventions.
1948	Between 1948 and 1954, takes charge of production technology classes at companies across Japan. He begins to question the nature of plant layout during a production technology course held at Hitachi, Ltd.'s Fujita plant.

1950	After studying and reflecting on the problem of layout, he perfects and implements a method based on a coefficient of ease of transport at Furkawa Electric's Copper Refinery in Nikko. The first stages of SMED are birthed during analysis work at a press at Toyo Kogyo. This involves splitting set-up operations into internal and external set-ups.
1951	He encounters and then applies statistical quality control in his role as Head of the Education Department.
1954	A representative from Toyota Motor Co., Morita Masanobu, attends a production technology course taught by Shigeo Shingo at Toyoda Automatic Loom. Morita Masanobu applies what he learned during the course and achieves striking results when they are applied at Toyota. As a result, Shigeo Shingo becomes one of the first consultants Toyota Motor Company hires. This marks the beginning of his in-depth involvement with Toyota and the Toyota Production System.
1955	Assumes control of industrial engineering and factory improvement training at the Toyota Motor Co. for both its employees and parts suppliers (100 companies). Is impressed by the separation of workers and machines while observing multiple machine operations at the first production technology training course at Toyota Motor Corp.

1956	Took charge of a three year study from 1956 to 1958 concerning ship building at Mitsubishi Shipbuilding's Nagasaki shipyards. During this study he implements his second revolutionary accomplishment by creating a system for hull assembly of 65,000 ton super-tankers after being told such a system would be impossible. Shigeo Shingo succeeds in cutting ship building time from four months down to two and in the process establishes a new world record. Within a year all ship yards in Japan are using his method.
1957	While at Mitsubishi Shipbuilding's Hiroshima shipyards he doubles the work rate of an engine bed planer by constructing a spare table. He conducts advance set-up operations on it and changes work piece and table together. This foreshadows a crucially decisive conceptual element of SMED, that of shifting internal activities to external activities.
1959	After 14 years with the Japan Management Association, Shigeo Shingo leaves to found the Institute of Management Improvement. The Institute is still in operation today.
1960-90	Dr. Shingo continued his work until a fully realized SMED system was developed. His system of achieving zero quality defects (poka-yoke) eventually saw some plant operations going over two years with *zero defects*. He continued working, consulting, and lecturing around the world until his death in 1990.

A Book Discussion on Kaizen and the Art of Creative Thinking

The following is a conversation between Norman Bodek, credited with being the 'Godfather of Lean', and David S. Veech, Executive Director of the Institute for Lean Systems in Louisville, Kentucky. The discussion centers on Dr. Shigeo Shingo's book, *Kaizen and the Art of Creative Thinking*.

BODEK: What David and I have in common is to teach people how to have an advanced suggestion system, a new way of getting people involved. This is the often-misunderstood element of Toyota's success — developing and empowering people to be creative on the job. This latest book by Dr. Shingo provides us with original insight into this creative element.

VEECH: I think the most important thing for managers to do is to teach their people how to solve problems.

BODEK: Ah, but you see, we don't often teach that do we?

VEECH: That's because we haven't taught our managers how to be teachers.

BODEK: Yes, and this is part of what Dr. Shingo's book is about. He has gone through and taken out the best ideas from all of the great teachers of continuous improvement and developed a thinking methodology, a step–by–step approach that he calls The Scientific Thinking Mechanism.

VEECH: What I think this book offers more than anything else is a window into how Dr. Shingo's mind actually worked; how he actually brought new thinking to different processes. Having that shared insight and additional information is priceless. Norman, you did the same thing when you published Taiichi Ohno's books like *Toyota Production System*. These books tell so much about what the architects of the Toyota Production System actually did, and how they thought about what they did. It really reveals some of their hidden art.

The more understanding we have about the hidden art of these great thinkers, the more likely we are able to apply it ourselves.

BODEK: Dr. Shingo taught 3,000 Toyota engineers the fundamentals of process thinking, which he covers thoroughly in this book. Like Dr. Shingo, David, you are teaching a thinking system, or an idea system.

VEECH: I am. I'm teaching a suggestion system that comes partly from Maasaki Imai's work, Kaizen, and partly from the history of the Toyota Production System. But what I'm doing, what I'm teaching, is primarily that the new suggestion system is the teaching tool for problem solving skills for the workforce.

When you get somebody with a great idea, what you really have is someone who is ready and willing to learn. When they come in and tell you about their idea, they are the perfect vessel for learning. You've got their full involvement, their full engagement, and their full attention.

We as leaders in organizations can totally crush that by saying, "I don't have time for this right now," or even, "It's an okay idea." We can also crush it by having them fill out an overly complex suggestion form and sticking in a suggestion box. Or we can embrace our responsibility as teachers and listen to the idea, and let them do an internal analysis themselves of whether the idea is good or not.

And if they say, "You know, that's probably not a good idea," that's okay, because then they're going to go and refine it and they're going to come back to you.

So with a focus on what you and I are doing with Quick & Easy Kaizen, some of the organizations that we're working with are introducing simplified forms. The forms capture ideas quickly, and then the team member, with help either from peers, a team leader, or a specific coach, works through that idea himself rather than sending the idea off to some black hole of engineering.

Dr. Shingo instructs us to keep the analysis, and hence the learning, at that team member level so they can have the benefit of going through that problem solving process and actually reaching a solution on their own.

BODEK: You just brought up something brilliant, two points we have to talk about and work on.

One is, 'that moment' a great learning moment for the manager and the worker. And if the manager looks at the worker and thinks, "How do we use this for the worker's education," that's the key. How do we look at this for the benefit and the growth of the worker?

That was brilliant but the next thing in this area is defining the ultimate role of the manager. The manager should really have only a few key roles, because a well-managed company needs less managing.

A Socio-Technical System, something Toyota is now slowly applying, doesn't need managers except as people that are visionaries to give direction. So what is the role of the manager in a lean system?

VEECH: It's to teach. And that doesn't mean we've got to pull people together in a classroom and show slides. It's interacting every day with folks doing the work.

BODEK: Just last week, I was at a plant and saw a worker at a powder coating operation. I looked and saw paint billowing out of the painting booth and all over the floor. I asked, "Why is that happening? It's making the place filthy and will get into everyone's lungs."

The worker replied, "Well, because there's a leak inside the booth."

And I asked him, "What can you do to fix it?"

He replied, "All we've got to do is solder it and cover it."

But we never ask the worker. He's just told to show up and do his job.

VEECH: That's right, and they're doing they're job. They're doing what they're asked to do.

BODEK: Yes. So let's further this aspect you have just brought out. The real role of the manager is to take that magic moment when the worker comes up with an idea and...

VEECH: Teach them how to analyze the idea, which is usually a countermeasure to the problem someplace. Most of the ideas that people have are to solve the problems they have at work. The idea is a countermeasure.

We have to understand what problem the idea is going to address first. We have to analyze the problem to make sure that the idea is actually going to solve it at its root cause. It's kind of working backwards a little bit. We normally see a problem first and have to come up with the countermeasure. Here, in this quick and easy suggestion system, we get the idea first and, as managers, we discover the problem with the help of the team member.

BODEK: This is wonderful. This is where Dr. Shingo is instructing us to teach managers, because at this point managers are always looking for big ideas and unfortunately, managers think that it's their job to come up with the solutions, so they rarely ask the worker.

Managers are always looking for the big solutions. However, Dr. Shingo is teaching us to take this opportunity as managers and break it down into very small, workable, and understandable steps.

VEECH: That's part of the analysis. Whenever we analyze something, we're going to break it into something smaller that we can understand a little bit easier.

BODEK: In Japan, they're doing this. The average worker in Japan submits and implements 24 improvement ideas per year and saves their company $4000 per year from their ideas.

VEECH: I'm consulting at Skier's Choice, where they're using a Lean improvement activity sheet that simply identifies what the problem looks like before a solution is applied and then what it will look like after. It pretty much simplifies the suggestion system process.

Workers make a one-page suggestion report on the solutions they implement themselves based on the values of the company. So the company has spent time teaching the things that are important; ensuring before you make this change you check with the people who you're going to impact, and make sure that everybody gets a chance to have some input.

Our clients have done thousands of these. One even has a little low-hanging fruit tree in their building where people post ideas or problems. Others look at the ideas or problems, pick that "low hanging fruit" from the tree, and go implement the idea in their area, or solve the problem. It's just an encouraging way to foster better communications.

BODEK: We have to begin to really trust people, to give them an opportunity to learn every day on the job and to give the worker the responsibility to make the product right. If I make a mistake, I'm going to learn from that mistake. But management doesn't want me to make mistakes which is very shortsighted. Management might as well say, "Don't make mistakes — don't learn!"

You just opened something very powerful for us and we have to discuss it. How do we train managers to teach workers this process… this process of discovering the problems around them and giving them the opportunity to grow on the job from their implemented ideas?

VEECH: We've got to teach people how to think about what they're doing. It's not enough just to go in and tell people, "Well, you're empowered now. Think about your work, too."

You can't expect people to do anything unless you deliberately teach them what they need to know.

That doesn't mean that you don't have a brilliant workforce already. You probably have folks that can do this without a second's delay. But in order to incorporate this thinking into a sustainable lean system, then you've got to have a structured way to teach, a structured way to support, and a structured way to implement.

BODEK: Dr. Shingo was always direct and uncomplicated. These models presented in the book are the missing link to driving this kind of success we are talking about today.

VEECH: It is brilliant, but I think some of your readers are going to be challenged by some of the stories in the book and say, "Well, I can see why Dr. Shingo decided to do the weld on one side of that washer plate and not both sides. But I make plastic parts. What does this have to do with me?"

And that's one of the points of resistance that we encounter all the time. "Yeah, that's great for those guys, but what about me? I'm different."

BODEK: Everybody says that. But, Dr. Shingo is trying to give us the foundational elements of problem solving; to take us through the four purposes of improvement, and the 12 steps of idea generation and he has delivered. I want to break this down very simply so that we go back to what you just said, which was so powerful. It is the manager's job to teach the worker how to think, how to grow from his own ideas, and to let the worker become their own teacher. In other words, let them grow from their own struggles.

We have to widen people's jobs. That's what a Socio–Technical System does. We have to widen people's roles and responsibilities and to have them understand more of the business. One of the most important roles the manager has is to bring out the best in people, or else we don't need managers. We need to help make superior people – they are superior as technicians on what they do but it is about growing that knowledge.

228

VEECH: We must have leaders designing systems that can draw learning energy from all team members. The role of a manager should be improving. Remember Imai's box? He's got improvement on top and maintenance on the bottom along with the amount of time people at various levels of the organization should spend on one versus the other. Senior managers should spend just about all of their time on improvement.

But what we have, especially in Western companies, are senior managers spending most of their time fire fighting, waiting for a problem to show up and then going out and solving the problem. And that's a big issue too, because we've got a whole generation of leaders and managers who think their job is to solve problems, when their actual job should be teaching the people who discovered those problems, how to solve it themselves.

And that, I think, is going to be the big one to overcome for us as a society.

BODEK: Well, we're going to do it. Mr. Ohno gave us a great statement; I started off talking about that today. Mr. Ohno said, "You only ask and you don't tell people what to do... even if you know the answer." This is what Socrates did as a teacher.

VEECH: You're right. The great teachers have always asked questions.

BODEK: If the manager's job is to be the problem solver, then he's going to be fully occupied solving problems. But if he disseminates this to every worker, then he has nothing to do with solving problems, other than to teach workers how to do it. This is the real essence of Toyota's success.

VEECH: We learned at the Toyota North American Kaizen Conference that the three most important tools in Kaizen are string, cardboard, and tape. An operator can do anything with string, cardboard, and tape; they can make something and make mistakes without spending a ton of money. They can redo things, model things, try things out, and experiment. Once you get the design right, then you send it off to the engineering team and they can make something out of sheet metal or something like that.

BODEK: Let's keep moving forward on this, because managers today still feel that they're paid to be problem solvers. They don't want to give up their turf; they're afraid.

VEECH: I think the problem there is that most managers don't know the work well enough to be effective problem solvers because they're so detached from the actual work. Even the good ones who go out and have great relationships with their employees still don't have that intimate knowledge of what is an effective solution. Even though we have made these managers expect to have this role of problem solver, they're not really the right people. So we've got to get them to engage the workforce, where the skill really is, where the people really know what the problems are and which solutions will work. We must develop that link with the people who are actually doing the work.

BODEK: To what extent is it still applied at Toyota today?

VEECH: My most detailed knowledge comes from the Georgetown plant, of course, where I have many colleagues and friends who still work there. After much observation, I think the largest challenge is too many team leaders working the floor every day instead of being team leaders. They're not coaches anymore, they become production workers. They're fully engaged in productive work leaving little time to focus on improvement.

I was at Power Train (Toyota's Engine Plant in Georgetown) a few months ago and got to walk through a couple of operations with one of the employees, and he showed me some of the things that they were doing internally. I know the people are still engaged, they are still highly skilled, and their leaders are listening to them. So that's already a big plus.

What I recommend for anybody who wants to try this out is to run a participation-focused suggestion system for at least five years. I know nobody wants to wait that long but you are building a sustainable model and it takes time.

At Georgetown they started in 1989. In 1994, they had a 96% participation rate. The numbers of raw ideas kept going up until 1999, but their participation rate never hit 96% again. At that maximum participation rate, companies need to tweak the suggestion system to focus on something different.

The idea is to change the focus from participation, where you're trying to teach everybody how to navigate the system, to one on learning, where you have to have more challenging problems. This means you're going to have a more restrictive suggestion system. Fewer things are going to be eligible for the rewards and benefits of the suggestion system, but it's still going to be focused on problems that team members can solve.

BODEK: You keep it simple. People are excited and the focal point is on growing. If people understand this, the idea system could be the beginning of their college education. You just ask your team members, give them an actual support system and they'll run with it. I like what we're doing, David, because of what the this system does; it provides a college education on the job. They have the opportunity to grow on the job.

David, tell us why you think this book is so valuable to America.

VEECH: I think this book is valuable because it shows us more about how to think, in a systematic method, about our work. It also demands that we really know what's going on. Most of us assume that we do... but we don't. This book keeps it simple and straightforward, and if people recognize the power of asking questions and asking for help, then there are no limits to the creativity and energy you can create in your workforce.

BODEK: This is really what's missing but thankfully Dr. Shingo provides us with an answer on how to structure the improvement process so it will go forward within a company. We've never addressed that level before. We've been provided with specific tools like SMED, 5S, JIT, and TPM, but we've never been provide the framework that teaches people how to solve problems – this is why this book is so influential and inspiring. The beautiful part of this book is that, all the way back in 1958, Dr. Shingo was providing the fundamentals to 'Toyota learning', to go after the facts.

VEECH: So many organizations say they're really data–driven organizations; they've got Six Sigma black belts and they're doing great stuff with them. These are people who are supposed to be able to handle all of this data. But I haven't found too many organizations that are really fact based. The discipline associated with Six Sigma is very powerful for sustaining gains, but I think we can do so much more if we get everybody generating facts instead of guesses.

BODEK: Six Sigma is basically TQC with black belts. Now, the black belts are very clever, but TQC was taught to every worker. The difference is that Six Sigma is not taught to every worker.

VEECH: That's my biggest problem with it, too. It's a problem solving methodology that they're reserving for a few people instead of everybody.

BODEK: The Japanese also continue to use Quality Control Circles, I don't know why we don't do that in America.

VEECH: I know why we're not doing it in America; because Quality Control Circles were all about a process and all we seem to care about are results. So when a manager can't have a quality circle that saves him $100,000 in a year, he's not going to spend the $60,000 on overtime that it's going to cost him. QC Circles were designed to teach small groups of people how to collectively solve problems. They used real problems as the teaching tools. What American businesses focused on when Joseph Juran brought QC Circles home, was the potential savings the teams generated. Results, not process. When we didn't get the advertised results, we pulled the plug.

BODEK: I like that. That's the 'whole thing' that we have to work on; the 'whole results', the 'whole profit.' I'm working with one company, and all they can think about is profits, and the company is melting and disappearing, instead of focusing on the process. Focus on the right process, and you get the right results.

Let's look at Dr. Shingo's Analytical Thinking Diagram for a few moments.

VEECH: I understand that the subject is who, the object is what we're looking for, the method is how, the space is where and the time is when. Toyota still uses this simple organizational tool they call the 5 W's and 1 H. What's missing, and what I think Dr. Shingo is trying to capture in the diagram, is why. I think, though, that it's part of avoiding ambiguities — understanding a little bit more. That takes us back to knowing instead of guessing.

I think Dr. Shingo is trying to say that we lack the quantitative knowledge of who is actually affecting what, so we obscure the subject and the object of the problem. And if your definition of the subject and the object is not truly accurate, it doesn't matter what method or what constraints there are, you're going to get a bad solution. The problem is going to come back.

I think what he succeeds most at is showing us how to clearly communicate quantitatively. We must have true knowledge of the subject and object, not just guesses, not just assumptions. We've really got to know that.

BODEK: That's why he says we have to avoid ambiguity, we must have true knowledge.

VEECH: Dr. Shingo also talks about 4 purposes of improvement, listing them as 1) Increasing productivity, 2) Improving quality, 3) Cutting time, and 4) Cutting cost. If we can make our team members' work more interesting or easier, we are very likely to achieve all four of these purposes of improvement. If we can do that AND improve the problem solving skills of those same team members, now we have sustainable improvement. This requires that we focus again on process not on results.

We have to acknowledge the most important processes are the ones we adopt as our standard approach to problem solving. We build this into our standardized work system, so that every time someone has an idea, they go through this process of analysis, synthesis, and evaluation. It doesn't have to be complicated and it doesn't have to be time-consuming. But it does have to begin with the team members, who need the skill and the confidence to start sharing their ideas. We still have a long way to go, but a book like this definitely provides direction.

List of Figures

Chapter Three

CHAPTER SIX

List of Tables

Index

A

T

Publications from Enna and PCS Inc.

Enna and PCS Inc. provide companies with publications that help achieve excellence in operations. Enna and PCS Inc. support your efforts to internalize process improvement allowing you to reach your vision and mission. These materials are proven to work in industry. Call toll-free (866) 249-7348 or visit us on the web at www.enna.com to order or request our free product catalog.

Training Materials and Books

The Idea Generator, Quick and Easy Kaizen

The book discusses the Kaizen mind set that enables a company to utilize its resources to the fullest by directly involving all of its manpower in the enhancement and improvement of the productivity of its operations.
ISBN 978-0971243699 | 2001 | $47.52 | Item: **902**

The Strategos Guide to Value Stream & Process Mapping

The Strategos Guide to Value Stream and Process Mapping has proven strategies and helpful tips on facilitating group VSM exercises and puts VSM in the greater Lean context. With photos and examples of related Lean practices the book focuses on implementing VSM, not just drawing diagrams and graphs.
ISBN 978-1-897363-43-0 | 2007 | $47.00 | Item: **905**

Quick and Easy Kaizen Training Package

Quick and Easy Kaizen is the most effective and powerful way to implement a practical and sustainable employee-led improvement system by encompassing the often-ignored human (employee) side of Lean manufacturing. Enna's Quick and Easy Kaizen is authored by Norman Bodek and made popular by his award winning Shingo Prize book, *Quick and Easy Kaizen: The Idea Generator*.
ISBN 978-1-897363-37-9 | 2006 | $699.99 | Item: **18**

Kaikaku, The Power and Magic of Lean

Kai ka ku are Japanese characters meaning a 'transformation of the mind,' Norman Bodek brings his vast cross-cultural experience in Japanese manufacturing systems to American industry and creates proven results. With his first-hand knowledge of Lean Manufacturing origins, Norman Bodek chronicles his introduction to Lean in an easy to read, conversational style text.
ISBN 978-0971243668 | 2006 | $47.52 | Item: **901**

JIT is Flow

Hirano's *5 Pillars of the Visual Workplace* and *JIT Implementation Manual* were classics. They contained detailed descriptions of techniques and clear instructions. However, Hirano's books were difficult to adapt to many sectors. This book highlights the depth of the thought process behind Hirano's work. The know-how that is contained in this book is extremely useful. The clarity which Hirano brings to JIT/Lean and the delineation of the principles involved will be invaluable to every leader and manager aiming for business excellence.
ISBN 978-0971243613 | 2006 | $47.52 | Item: **903**

Rebirth of American Industry

We had a certain amount of sadness as we read of the bankruptcy of Delphi Corporation, and the losses and downsizing of General Motors and Ford. The very purpose of this book is to provide modern managers with specific guidelines to be internationally competitive. The book traces the evolution of manufacturing management along two lines: That pioneered by Henry Ford, then furthered by Toyota to its modern level of success; versus that originated by Alfred Sloan and others at General Motors still in practice in most American companies today.
ISBN 978-0971243637 | 2005 | $47.52 | Item: **904**

All You Gotta Do Is Ask

So, after all the committees, review panels, and head scratching, your company has finally started its Lean transformation. *All You Gotta Do Is Ask* explains how to promote a tidal swell of ideas from your employees. This easy-to-read book will show you why it is important to have a good idea system, how to set one up, and what it can do for you, your employees, and your organization.
ISBN 978-0971243651 | 2005 | $47.52 | Item: **906**

To order: Enna Products Corp. 1602 Carolina St., Unit B3, Bellingham, WA 98

Overview of Lean Training Package

This package has been designed to create the understanding needed to commit to a Lean Transformation. Make the most of our introductory Lean package by training all your staff in the principles of Lean Manufacturing. Included with this package is a factory flow simulation exercise to demonstrate the concepts of Lean in a real-time exercise. This comprehensive training package is action oriented to ensure successful learning and communication of Lean Manufacturing principles. ISBN 978-0-973750-92-8 | 2006 | $349.99 | Item: **11**

5S Training Package

Our 5S Solution Packages will help your company create a sustainable 5S program that will turn your shop floor around, and put you ahead of the competition. All of the benefits that come from Lean Manufacturing are built upon a strong foundation of 5S. The success or failure of all improvement initiatives can be traced to the robustness of 5S programs. Enna's solution packages will show you how to implement and sustain an environment of continuous improvement.

Version 1: ISBN 978-0-973750-90-4 | 2005 | $429.99 | Item: **12**
Version 2: ISBN 978-1-897363-25-6 | 2006 | $429.99 | Item: **17**
Version 1: Sort, Straighten, Sweep, Standardize, and Sustain.
Version 2: Sort, Set In Order, Shine, Standardize, and Sustain

To Order:

Phone, fax, email, or mail to Enna Products Corporation ATTN: Order Processing, 1602 Carolina Street, Unit B3, Bellingham, WA, 98229 USA. Phone: (866) 249-7348, Fax: (905) 481-0756, Email: info@enna.com. Send checks to this address. We accept all major credit cards.

International Orders:

Phone, fax, email, or mail to Enna Products Corporation ATTN: Order Processing, 1602 Carolina Street, Unit B3, Bellingham, WA, 98229 USA. For international calls, Telephone number: +1 (360) 306-5369, Email: info@enna.com, and Facsimile number: +1 (905) 481-0756.

Notice:

All prices are in US dollars and are subject to change without notice.